ICES ITALIA

ICES ITALIA

LINDA TUBBY

Photography by Jean Cazals

PAVILION

Dedicated to my sons Dan and Ben and my friend Ruth Prentice, with love

CONTENTS

THE SNOW AND ICE AGE

There is a lack of credibility in many of the stories surrounding the origins of Italian ices. Most are based on myths and legends but a number are plausibly linked to real historic events and provide a fascinating trail through a variety of countries. Like many inventions, it is often difficult to pinpoint one source or inventor, or even specific dates for that matter. Looking into the concept of the "discovery" of gelato, I found myself following the most tenuous of links and unearthed some fascinating stories.

One tale talks of the Venetian traveller and writer, Marco Polo, bringing the concept of frozen ices back to Italy from China. It is said, but hotly disputed, that he observed the Chinese using ice and fermented milk in a way that would later be developed in Italy during the 16th century. The Chinese knew about the usefulness of harvesting and storing snow and ice and had been freezing things for thousands of years. The widespread use of this natural cooler, teamed with exotically flavoured syrups, was also being enjoyed before the time of Marco Polo in India and Persia. Arab traders travelled with this knowledge, and settled the habit firmly with the Sicilians, who later perfected the art. The indication is that the first sorbetto was simply a loosely frozen, highly aromatic and sweet drink.

Long before Marco Polo, the Romans knew all about how to make full use of the seasonal harvest of snow and ice. Iced drinks – *bevande ghiacciate* – were part of everyday life in Rome. Slave runners carried huge blocks of icy snow down from the mountains not far from the city. Storing snow for use throughout the hot summers was a necessity. It was used to add a chill to the warm, heavy wine, making it more palatable. Snow also supplied a treat of pure icy slush, which could then be flavoured with fruit and honey syrups. Emperor Nero Claudius had an unquenchable liking for ice-cold wine. The drinking vessel used at the time was revolutionary – it had two chambers, the outer packed with snow and the inner chamber containing the drink itself.

Towards the end of the 16th century a number of people in Naples were playing with the idea of freezing. One scientist in particular, Giambattista Della Porta, was forging ahead with his own experiments using cooling techniques that worked well enough to freeze diluted wine. The temperature of water drops when salt is added and dissolved into it – initially saltpetre was used. It was later found that normal salt crystals did the job perfectly

Right (clockwise from top left): Classic Italy: a fountain in the Piazza Navona, Rome; an old-fashioned gelato maker; the historic Piazza della Cisterna, San Gimignano; a shrine in Rome, stuffed with prayers.

well. This process of freezing was made all the more powerful by rotating a vessel filled with liquid buried in a snow and salt mixture called *salamoia*.

Many began to make use of this growing knowledge, including Bernardo Buontalenti – a multi-talented Florentine artist, designer of buildings, firework festivals, feasts for the Medici family and possibly the instigator of the post-Italian Renaissance gelato boom. He and his recipes were the talk of the Italian glitterati and he was requested to take charge of organizing luxurious banquets to impress the guests of the Medici who frequently visited from other countries. To this day, Italians pay homage to him by making a gelato named after him (see p.104). A *Buontalenti* is an egg enriched custard gelato, sweetened with honey and flavoured with wine. It is said he was the first to add eggs to milk to produce a custard base.

Just outside Florence, Buontalenti built Pratolini – a summer residence for the Grand Duke – and installed snow pits in the grounds of the villa. These were covered with an insulating pyramid of thatch designed to store icy snow carried down from the mountains for a full year without melting away. (Snow when compacted into blocks lasts a very long time.) He also had pits built in the Boboli gardens and around the walls of Florence to store snow and ice for sale to the general public who by now, just like the nobility, wanted an on-hand supply during the scorching summer months.

Above: Gelato preparation at Gelateria di "Piazza".

Concessions giving permission to collect and store snow and ice were being sold to the highest bidder. It seemed in everyone's interests therefore to promote the new idea that was exciting the fashionable rich of the day. Iced follies became the big thing at grand banquets. Vast visual displays were increasingly over-the-top, with crushed ice and snow the basis for these magnificent arrangements. Showy pyramids and obelisks of seasonal fruits encased in ice, strewn with tangles of heavily scented orange blossoms, sweet jasmine and scented roses, bedecked the tables on these glamorous occasions.

Due to the huge popularity of ice and snow it made more economic sense to take ice from the local lakes and rivers, or to dig reservoirs close to the villas of the nobility and, when they filled with water and froze over in the coldest months, carve out the blocks of ice and put those into storage.

By the late 17th century Antonio Latini, an official who organized and supervised food and entertainment for the Spanish Prime Minister of Naples, started to write about entertaining and cooking, and included details on how to make ices. He masterminded the making of beautifully ornate iced serving bowls, *vasi di ghiaccio*, made from moulded ice containing fruits suspended inside a thinner layer of ice. He also wrote quite specific recipes for frozen flavoured ices embedded with fruit, and for sweetened milk-based ones, which were lightly frozen, then moulded into brick shapes

Above: Spectacular iced desserts.

and frozen hard. Eggs, cream and even butter were used in milk-based ices to enrich the mixture already scented with orange flower water, cinnamon and vanilla. Meanwhile, the not so wealthy population of Naples had once again adopted the ancient Roman idea of putting syrups onto snow. These were called *neve* ("snow") and were sold on the streets, but in comparison to the grand iced arrangements at the banquets of the rich it was all relatively frugal.

From the late 17th century the craze for ices was spreading to the rest of Europe with the help of the now iconic Parisian café in the Rue de l'Ancienne Comédie – Café Procope – which is named after its one-time Sicilian owner Francesco Procopio Dei Coltelli. He went to Paris with some knowledge of how to make sorbetto, and it is believed that his grandfather, also Francesco, had designed a machine that improved the texture of ice flavoured with fruit and sweetened with honey. He was granted a royal patent to sell his ices exclusively. A century later, Guiseppe Tortoni, another Italian, was running a café in Paris, and by then the use of cream in ices was commonplace. His son's recipe for Biscuit Tortoni, which is still made, became very famous (see p.126).

By the late 18th century a new and widespread belief was emerging, supporting and encouraging the health-giving benefits of snow and ice to treat all ills. Dr. Filippo Baldini, a

respected Neapolitan physician, wrote a book promoting the health benefits of sorbette. Everyone was now into the sorbetto craze in the belief that this icy palate cleanser would counteract over-indulgence in rich food and alcohol. Many of these ices were called *aromatici*, and were designed by herbalists using beneficial ingredients. Also on the menu were pretty much all the flavours that are in evidence today – strawberry, amerene (the sour cherry), pistachio, peach, watermelon, coffee and chocolate, to name but a few.

By the late 19th century, making artificial ice and snow was becoming a common occurrence to augment the natural supply. Natural ice and snowfall had managed to keep step with the demand for hundreds of years, but the increase in popularity meant that a more consistent supply was needed. Artificial ice, however, was expensive to produce and was now being made from distilled water that froze to crystal-clearness. Iced desserts were becoming ever more elaborate using wildly ornamental shapes that reflected the opulence of the age.

What emerges from the little-recorded history that does exist, is that while the Italians may not have originated the concept, they are undeniably responsible for the development, the subsequent emigration and the reigning popularity of ices – the world's favourite comfort food.

Opposite: *Zuccotto* at Gelateria Combattenti in San Gimignano (see p.145). **Top:** *Spumoni* and *Pezzi Duri* at Gelateria Petrini, Rome. **Bottom:** Colourful *Pezzi Duri* at Palazzo de Freddo di Giovanni Fassi, Rome. **Overleaf:** Gelateria Giolitti, Rome.

THE ART OF GELATO

With 290,000 tons of artisan-made gelato produced each year the Italians don't just make gelato, they have a passion for it. The gelato-maker is known as a *gelataio* by the general buying public. The one who balances the ingredients to invent and create brand new recipes often prefers to be called a *"gelatiere"*, the head chef in the world of gelato.

The Italian, artisan gelato-maker's day starts around dawn. Each batch of softly scoopable gelato and sorbetto are made daily in small quantities, with the most popular flavours being replenished throughout the day. High standards are required to create a top-quality product. Gelato-makers use only the best seasonal ingredients, which are bought fresh each day, along with back-up flavourings using the best quality storecupboard (pantry) ingredients available. They have true dedication to their craft, as in most parts of Italy gelato-making is almost a year-round business with usually only a small break in the winter. Gelato is not just for tourists, it's what the locals have always wanted, and they don't just indulge in a cone or two – they buy a kilo at a time to take away.

The question people always ask is why Italian gelato is so different from its kissing cousin the ice cream. For a start, gelato doesn't mean "iced cream", in Italian it means "frozen" and comes from *gelare* meaning "to freeze over". Some describe eating Italian ices as purification of the palate. Fundamentally gelato is different because it is served at a warmer temperature than ice cream, and because it is made freshly in small batches on a daily basis the flavours retain a wonderful purity. Gelato is a relatively modern term – the name used before was *mantecato*, a word derived from the whipping action in the churning process.

The gelato-maker is a scientist, knowing how to use the right combination of sugars and other ingredients to transform a gelato into something sublime. Skimmed milk powder has a high viscosity and when used helps hold the ingredients in suspension and hinders ice crystals building up. Cream added to a gelato mixture is in need of strong flavourings to counteract the richness – it's this balance that needs skill in the creation of the perfect gelato. In some cases, they will use a little natural stabilizer made from carob bean gum to prevent large ice crystals forming. This is sometimes necessary in a fruit mixture with a high water content. Combined with a vast knowledge of temperature effects, and by how much the volume increases through churning, it certainly is a real art.

Right: Sergio Dondole at his Gelateria di "Piazza" in San Gimignano.

Above: Gelateria Pellacchia 1900, Rome.

In an artisan gelateria the product is displayed in large glass-fronted display cabinets that are kept at a temperature of –14°C (7°F). By the time the gelati and sorbette are scooped into cones and taken outside to eat, they are at just the right temperature to maximise the wonderful flavour and texture. There are still some gelaterias that retain the old-style round stainless steel tubs with lids (see left), but now it's more common to be able to see and inspect all the various flavours piled high in open rectangular stainless steel tubs.

In large establishments a cashier sits at a till like a wooden pulpit, and you will be expected to have decided how many flavours (*gusti*) you want to pay for before presenting yourself at the gelato counter with your receipt. This means having a good look first at all the possibilities on offer. If the gelato is good, there is often a long queue of people all waiting eagerly. For the Italians there is no right or wrong time to consume gelato – 10am to midnight and beyond.

I love the way all Italian gelato is served. They use a special type of flat scoop (see right), and each flavour is plastered onto the cone or into a paper cup. Up to four flavours at a time is quite normal, but two or three are more common. Italians are also partial to *panna montata*, the whipped cream added to the top of a gelato-filled cone. A large tub always sits behind the counter, softly whipped.

If you have never made ices before I can promise you will be converted. To produce the finest gelato and sorbetto at home, with or without a machine, is simple and one of life's absolute pleasures. Like the Italians I have come to believe that ices were never intended to be served frozen hard, or kept in the freezer for lengthy periods of time. They should be served when soft and voluptuous. There is no need to add anything but the purest produce to your mixtures. Make full use of what the seasons bring and choose organic where possible.

I like the different texture each ingredient brings to Italian ices. I often find a sugar content that makes the perfect sorbetto consistency is just too sweet for many tastes. There is a fine line between just sweet enough and over-sweet. If not enough sugar is added to a sorbetto mixture sometimes the texture will be grainy – I quite like this effect depending on the main ingredient and often prefer it as the flavours pack more of a punch rather than vying for attention against a sugar overload.

Texture is controllable for the home gelato-maker. If too much sugar has been added to the mixture, freezing will be impaired, while too much alcohol will prevent ice crystals forming. Just the right iced texture that is perfect for you can be timed to coincide with when you want to eat your ice. I like to prepare a mixture and leave it unchurned in the refrigerator so that the flavours can mature. A few hours away from serving, I churn then freeze it for the time on the recipe, or "still freeze" (see p. 19) and again leave it in the freezer for the given time, so it is perfect for consumption. Depending on the recipe, I often get excited about eating the gelato or sorbetto straight "off" the machine when it's very soft, icy and delicious, or if "still freezing" it is often great eaten after the last aerating in the food processor.

Italian ice-making is a case of experimenting to find your own preferences for each recipe. Be warned, however – homemade gelato will not be instantly ready to eat if it accidentally gets over-frozen, in which case you should soften the gelato in the refrigerator before scooping. Each recipe gives instructions for this. Also, don't leave your gelato to defrost at room temperature; this varies so much you'll find it difficult to obtain the right consistency. If you are not quite ready to serve the gelato after softening, just pop the tub back into the freezer for re-chilling. Don't worry as it starts to soften – it should be easy to scoop, which means that it will be perfect to eat, so be brave.

Right: Italian gelato scoops, designed to plaster the layers of gelato or sorbetto onto a cone or into a cup.

GELATO RULES – STILL FREEZING

Still freezing is a method of producing ices without an ice cream machine. All you need to do is make sure the freezer is set at around -18°C (-0.4°F).

As the mixture starts to freeze the sugar content becomes concentrated and stays sticky and almost liquid, while the rest of the mixture starts to form ice crystals. Larger ice crystals will form the longer the mixture is left without agitating. If the mixture has a fat content, the fat forms globules as the mixture starts to freeze, which will keep the ice crystals apart, ensuring they don't grow so large. To create a smooth finish to the gelato and sorbetto, the ice crystals need to be constantly broken down and mixed with the rest of the ingredients to evenly distribute them throughout. This can be done using electric beaters or a hand whisk, but the secret lies in the final stage where you should use, if possible, a food processor. If you only have electric beaters, all is not lost, you'll simply end up with a slightly icier texture, which is still perfectly acceptable, but the mixture must be beaten four times over the course of the freezing process.

For the classic flavoured granita, the formed ice crystals are not broken down but are repeatedly forked over to keep the flaky chards of flavoured ice at just the right size. Due to the extra water in a granita, the crystallization process works well so it is much more ice-like. When found in gelaterias, granita looks slushy, like a rather wet sorbetto, and is continually churned in a circular, clear-sided machine.

How to still freeze gelato and sorbetto

Pour the prepared and chilled gelato or sorbetto mixture into a suitably sized rigid freezerproof container, ideally one with a clearance of about 3cm (1¼ inches) between the liquid and the top of the container, so when you use the beaters the mixture will not fly out.

Put the container uncovered in the coldest part of the freezer directly in contact with the open bars if possible. Freeze gelato for 2 hours, checking after 1½ hours, and sorbetto for 1½ hours, checking after the first hour. The quantities and ingredients for each recipe vary and affect precise freezing times.

The, using a fork, dig out the frozen edges and corners into the slushy centre and whisk the mixture with electric beaters or hand whisk until it is broken up and slushy. Repeat the freezing and whisking process again then refreeze until evenly firm but not frozen solid (about 2 hours). Next, transfer to a food processor and process for 1–2 minutes until smooth. Some of the sweeter mixes will be less firm after the third freezing, but this is fine, just as long as they are slushy. If the mixture clumps together during the final processing stop the motor, break up the lumps with a fork and continue processing.

Transfer the mixture into a freezerproof container and follow the instructions in the recipe regarding when to add the solid ingredients, and the final freezing timings, for a perfect result. Cover and label with the name and time it takes to soften in the refrigerator should it become over-frozen.

ICED DRINKS & GRANITE

Lemon Liqueur

LIMONCELLO

Available in bottles and made with lemons from the Amalfi Coast a liquore di limone *is rich with the tang of sun-ripened lemons. There is, however, nothing like making your own to get that full flavour. The pure alcohol is the preservative and it is kept in the freezer. Grappa can be used, but I prefer vodka. You will need two large, wide-necked jars with lids (about $^1/_2$ litre/1 pint each).*

Makes 1 litre/1$^1/_2$ pints

500 ml/16 fl oz/2 cups pure
    alcohol spirit, such as vodka
6 large lemons
350 g/12 oz/1$^3/_4$ cups caster
    (superfine) sugar
200 ml/7 fl oz/scant 1 cup
    pure still bottled water

Measure the alcohol into one of the jars. Using a vegetable peeler, take thin strips of peel from the lemons (avoiding the white pith) and add to the alcohol. Cover with the lid and leave in a cool dark place for 1$^1/_2$ months.

Meanwhile, squeeze the lemons to give about 250 ml/8 fl oz/1 cup of juice. Pour the juice into a small freezerproof container, label and freeze until the lemon-infused alcohol is ready to use.

When the lemon-infused alcohol is ready, put the sugar and water in a saucepan with the frozen lemon juice and heat gently to allow the sugar to dissolve and the juice to melt. Pour the mixture into a large jug (pitcher) to cool. Add the lemon-infused alcohol and the lemon peel from the jar, then stir, cover, and leave to stand overnight.

Strain the mixture into the two jars. Cover with the lids and store in a cool dark place for about 1 week.

Transfer the jars to the freezer and leave overnight or until the mixture thickens into a loose sludge (it never freezes completely). Use as you wish served in frozen glasses (put them in the freezer for 15 minutes beforehand). Alternatively, use in *Sgroppino* (opposite).

Lemon Sorbetto with Limoncello and Sparkling Wine

SGROPPINO CLASSICO AL LIMONE

Sometimes spelled scroppino *this frosty tipple is most common in Venice where they often whisk the ingredients together over ice. A mixture of homemade Lemon Sorbetto (p.58) and* Limoncello *(opposite) is blended to a delicious icy sludge. Usually, Prosecco is added to the mix, but I like to top the glass with this frothy fizz along with a shower of zesty lemon shavings. Serve in sugar-dipped glasses for even more sparkle (illustrated on p.21).*

Serves 4

3–4 tsp caster (superfine) sugar
  depending on your taste,
  plus extra for glass dipping
9 ice cubes
250 g/9 oz *Sorbetto di Limone*
  (p.58)
4 tbsp *Limoncello* (opposite)
  straight from the freezer
1 unwaxed lemon, rind shaved
  or grated
1 bottle of Prosecco, chilled

Put the glasses in the freezer for 15 minutes. Put the sugar, ice cubes, sorbetto and *Limoncello* in a blender and process until sludgy and all the ice is crushed.

Spread some sugar out on a plate and dip the ice-cold rims of the glasses into it to coat. Spoon in the sorbetto mixture and top with shaved or grated lemon rind. Pour in the Prosecco and serve immediately while it is still fizzing.

Blueberry Smoothie

FRAPPÈ AI MIRTILLI

Frappè *is a touch more sophisticated than* frullato – *it is less mid-morning and more of an afternoon venture for me. Italians love these smoothies at any time of the day and they choose any* gusti *or "scoops" (*gusto *means "taste") of gelato or sorbetto they fancy. Blended with chilled milk and whizzed up to an iced creamy drink, these smoothies are often thick enough to eat with a long spoon and then you can drink the last dregs from the bottom of the glass. Top with a little fresh fruit for extra goodness.*

Makes 1 large glass

3 scoops of Gelato di Mirtilli
   blueberry gelato (p.102), or
   any fruit, chocolate, coffee
   or vanilla flavoured gelato,
   or even a flavoured sorbetto
100 ml/3$^{1}/_{2}$ fl oz/generous
   $^{1}/_{3}$ cup chilled milk

Put all the ingredients into a blender and process until thick and frothy. Pour into a glass and serve.

Redcurrant Milkshake

FRULLATO AL SUCCO ROSSO

Frullato *makes a great pick-me-up. It consists of fresh fruit, whatever is ripe and luscious and, most importantly in season, along with chilled milk or yogurt, or even a mix of the two. All you do is throw everything into a blender with ice cubes and purée in short bursts until the ice is like snow and the mixture is flecked with little bits of fruit. This is '60s milk-bar-shake-meets-modern-day smoothie.*

Makes 1 large glass

6 ice cubes
150 ml/5 fl oz/$^{2}/_{3}$ cup chilled
   milk
60 g/2$^{1}/_{4}$ oz/$^{1}/_{2}$ cup redcurrants
1–2 tbsp acacia honey

Put the ice cubes and 2 tablespoons of the milk into a blender and process until the ice is broken up.

Add the redcurrants and honey and continue to blend until thick, pink, but still flecked with the fruit. Pour into a glass and serve.

Papaya Milkshake

FRULLATO DI PAPAYA

Papaya contains an enzyme that is a good cure for upset stomachs – it's an excellent digestive aid and brimful of vitamin C, as well as being rich in vitamin A and betacarotene. Delicious.

Makes 1 large glass

1 papaya
Juice of 1 lime
2 tsp caster (superfine) sugar
   (optional)
6 ice cubes
150 ml/5 fl oz/^{2}/₃ cup chilled
   milk

Cut the papaya in half lengthways and scoop out the seeds with a teaspoon and discard. Scoop the flesh from each half straight into a blender. Add lime juice and process until a purée forms.

Add sugar if using (taste and adjust if necessary), ice cubes and chilled milk and blend until smooth. Pour into a glass and serve.

Coffee Milkshake

FRULLATO MACCHIATO AL CAFFÈ

Italians love their coffee. This frullato *provides a caffeine kick and, when teamed with the brilliant yellow herbal liqueur Strega (meaning "witch"), is hard to beat.*

Makes 1 large glass

100 ml/3^1/₂ fl oz/generous ^{1}/₃
   cup espresso, cooled
6 tbsp double (heavy) cream
2 tbsp Strega
3 tsp caster (superfine) sugar,
   or to taste
8 ice cubes
Drinking chocolate, to dust

Put all the ingredients into a blender and process for 30 seconds. Pour into a glass, dust with drinking chocolate and serve.

Gelato with Coffee

AFFOGATO

Affogato *means "drowned", which is exactly what happens to the scoops of rich vanilla flavoured gelato when a shot of boiling hot espresso hits them. The creamy foam on top of a freshly brewed espresso is called* crema di caffe, *and it is this that holds the deep concentrated flavour that makes the best* affogato, *as everything melds together. For extra indulgence, add a scoop of* Bacio, *a rich chocolate gelato, along with the* Fior di Latte con Vaniglia *vanilla gelato.*

Serves 4

4 scoops *Fior di Latte con Vaniglia* vanilla gelato (p.106)
4 scoops *Bacio* rich chocolate gelato, made without nuts and meringue (p.89), optional
About 400 ml/14 fl oz/1¾ cups hot strong espresso, depending on size of glass or cup
Chocolate truffle sticks (see Suppliers p.159), to serve

Put the scoops of gelato of your choice into each glass or cup and top with hot freshly brewed espresso. Serve immediately with a chocolate truffle stick.

Iced Spritz

SPRITZ GHIACCIATO

Pomegranate juice is so fashionable right now due to its high vitamin C content. The idea for this recipe was given to me by Guiseppe Ruo of the Lanesborough Hotel in London. This iced version of a "Spritz" cocktail should be served as an aperitivo, *a lightly alcoholic little something before a meal.*

Serves 4–6

100 g/4 oz/½ cup caster (superfine) sugar
100 ml/3½ fl oz/generous ⅓ cup water
200 ml/7 fl oz/scant 1 cup pomegranate juice
100 ml/3½ fl oz/generous ⅓ cup Campari
Slices of orange
1 bottle of Prosecco, chilled

Put the sugar and water in a saucepan and heat gently to dissolve the sugar, about 4 minutes. Swirl the pan around to dislodge any crystals on the bottom, then transfer to a bowl to cool.

Half the pomegranates one at a time (to avoid losing any juice) and using a lemon squeezer or an electric juicer, extract as much juice as possible. It is tricky to get all the juice, as the juicy seeds are tightly packed within their skin, so it's best to give a final squeeze by hand. Pass the juice through a nylon sieve (strainer) set over a bowl to catch any bits and mix in the sugar syrup. Add the Campari.

Churn in an ice cream machine following the manufacturer's instructions, cover and freeze. Alternatively, still freeze using the method on p.19.

It will be ready after 4 hours but if it is frozen for longer and freezes hard, remove the lid and transfer to the refrigerator for 20–30 minutes to soften.

To serve, scoop into small balls and put into glasses, add a slice of orange and top with Prosecco.

Watermelon Granita

GRANITA DI ANGURIA

This is essence of summer when you choose a ripe luscious melon with deep red flesh. Always go for a good quality rich Pinot Grigio – the flavour needs to be intense as freezing can dull it. The Roman version of granita is called grattachecca *and is more like grated ice with flavoured syrup poured over. Granita is tricky for gelaterias to produce as the process makes it difficult to store without being in a higher temperature freezer, so commercially-made granita is more sloppy and icy, churned all day in a machine, like a loose sorbetto.*

Serves 6–8

150 g/5 oz/³/₄ cup caster
  (superfine) sugar
250 ml/9 fl oz/generous 1 cup
  rich white wine, such as a
  good quality Pinot Grigio
2.125 kg/4²/₃ lb ripe
  watermelon
Juice of ¹/₂ lemon

Put the sugar and wine in a saucepan and heat gently to allow the sugar to dissolve, about 4 minutes. Swirl the liquid around the pan to dislodge any sugar crystals still on the bottom, then remove from the heat and leave to cool.

Cut the watermelon into slices, reserving some slices for later (see note below) and remove the flesh from the skin, picking out any easy-to-remove pips as you go. Put the flesh into a food processor and process briefly. This is to loosen the pips not pulverise them. Tip into a sieve (strainer) and with the back of a ladle push all the flesh through. Discard the pips and grainy bits still left in the sieve.

When the wine syrup is cool add the watermelon pulp and lemon juice and stir. Pour the mixture into a freezerproof container, ideally a size that allows a liquid depth of about 3 cm/1 inch, and freeze for 2 hours.

Remove from the freezer and, using a fork, scrape the frozen mixture around the sides into the centre and re-freeze. After another 3 hours fork over again to get a nice flaky effect and serve. If keeping for longer transfer to a smaller, deeper container for easier storage. If it's left for longer and is frozen hard take it out of the freezer 15 minutes before you need it and fork over again before serving.

Tip: Keep some fine slices of watermelon in the refrigerator for decorating the granita if using as soon as it is ready.

GRANITA D'UVA FRAGOLINA

Late August brings in pendulous bunches of strawberry-crush-flavoured "Fragolini" grapes. They are black and bloomed and not much larger than a healthy blueberry. Andreas, my local speciality greengrocer who also supplies The River Café in London, brings them from Italy when they are in season. Try other flavoursome grape varieties as a substitute.

Serves 6–8

1 kg/2¼ lb "Fragolina" grapes
500 ml/16 fl oz/2 cups cold
  water
150 g/5 oz/¾ cup caster
  (superfine) sugar
Juice of 1 lemon

Take the grapes off their stalks and reserve about 24 in the freezer for decoration. Put the rest in a colander set over the sink and pour over a kettle of boiling water (this scalds off any dirt). Tip them straight into a pan with the cold water and sugar and heat gently for a few minutes to allow the sugar to dissolve. Increase the heat and when bubbles appear around the edge of the pan remove from the heat. Pour the contents of the pan into a bowl, cover with a cloth and leave overnight.

Strain the juice into a bowl. Put the grapes into a food processor and pulse very briefly to break them down slightly, not to purée. Tip into a nylon sieve (strainer) set over a bowl and, using a circular motion, push the grapes through with the back of a ladle. Discard anything left behind in the sieve.

Mix in the lemon juice, pour the mixture into a freezerproof container, ideally a size that allows a liquid depth of about 3 cm/1 inch, and freeze for 2 hours. Remove from the freezer and, using a fork, scrape the frozen edges into the centre then re-freeze. After 3 hours fork over again to get a nice flaky effect and serve. (If freezing for longer transfer to a smaller, deeper container for easy storage. If frozen hard transfer to the refrigerator for about 30 minutes and fork over again before serving.) Remove the reserved grapes for decoration from the freezer 30 minutes before serving and pop a few on top of each dish.

Espresso Granita with Whipped Cream

GRANITA DI CAFFÈ ESPRESSO CON PANNA

The wake up call of a coffee granita on a sleepy holiday makes living worthwhile, especially when topped with a large dollop of panna montata *softly whipped cream. Serve as an after-dinner palate cleanser to awaken the taste buds before the rich hit of a chocolate gelato scoop.*

Serves 6–8

500 ml/16 fl oz/2 cups freshly brewed very strong espresso

150 g/5 oz/^{3}/$_4$ cup caster (superfine) sugar

2 splashes of Italian hazelnut liqueur, such as Frangelico

250 ml/9 fl oz/generous 1 cup double (heavy) cream, softly whipped

Put the espresso and sugar in a saucepan and heat gently to allow the sugar to dissolve for 4 minutes. Increase the heat and boil for 3 minutes then transfer to a bowl and leave to cool completely.

Splash in the hazelnut liqueur and stir. Pour the mixture into a freezerproof container, ideally a size that allows a liquid depth of about 3 cm/1 inch. Freeze for about 3 hours until slushy. Remove from the freezer and, using a fork, scrape the frozen edges into the centre. Freeze for a further 3 hours, then fork over again to get a nice flaky effect and serve. If freezing for longer transfer to a smaller, deeper container for easy storage. If frozen hard transfer to the refrigerator for about 15 minutes and fork over again before serving.

Spoon some whipped cream onto each serving.

Almond Granita

GRANITA DI MANDORLE

*A classic from Sicily, Avola almonds (*mandorle*) are used for this quenching granita made with almond milk, which is soothing and cooling in the heat of the scorching summer. The "mandorle" goes right back to the Arab invasion of the island.*

Serves 8

400 g/14 oz/2²/3 cups blanched almonds

85 g/3¹/2 oz/scant ¹/2 cup caster (superfine) sugar

1 litre/1³/4 pints/4 cups water

4 tbsp rosewater

5 drops almond oil (see Suppliers p.159)

Process the almonds and sugar in a food processor until finely ground. Add 250 ml/9 fl oz/generous 1 cup water and process for a further 3 minutes until smooth.

Set a nylon sieve (strainer) over a bowl and pour in the liquid, pushing it through with the back of a ladle. Return the almond pulp to the processor with another 250 ml/9 fl oz/generous 1 cup water and process again for 3 minutes. Repeat this twice more then discard the almond pulp.

Pour the mixture into a freezerproof container, ideally a size that allows a liquid depth of about 3 cm/1 inch, and freeze for 1¹/2 hours. Remove from the freezer and, using a fork, scrape the frozen mixture around the sides into the centre and re-freeze. After another 1¹/2 hours fork over again to get a nice flaky effect. Repeat this once more then serve. If keeping for longer transfer to a smaller, deeper container for easier storage. If it is left for longer and is frozen hard take it out of the freezer 1 hour before you need it and fork over again, then if necessary put it back into the freezer for no more than 15 minutes before serving.

GRANITA DI MANDARINO E CARDAMOMO

Oranges (arance) *are grown throughout the southern part of Italy and there so many different varieties including the* Sanguigno *– just one of the blood oranges of Sicily. Oranges were first cultivated in Sicily by the Arabs, who brought them from Asia around the 9th and 10th centuries. The* manderino *appears in autumn (fall), which makes this a perfect Christmas palate cleanser between courses, served in tiny bowls or glasses.*

Serves 6–8

12 mandarin oranges

175 g/6 oz/scant 1 cup caster
   (superfine) sugar

8 cardamoms, bruised to split
   the skins

425 ml/14$^1/_2$ fl oz/generous
   1$^3/_4$ cups water

Juice of 1 lemon

Juice the mandarins and strain into a bowl. There will be 500 ml/ 16 fl oz/2 cups of juice. Put the sugar, cardamoms and water in a saucepan and heat gently to dissolve the sugar, about 4 minutes. Swirl the liquid around the pan to dislodge any sugar crystals still on the bottom, then remove from the heat, transfer to a bowl and leave to cool.

Strain the syrup through a sieve (strainer) into the mandarin juice and mix. Pour the mixture into a freezerproof container, ideally a size that allows a liquid depth of about 3 cm/1 inch, and freeze for 2 hours. Remove from the freezer and using a fork, scrape the frozen mixture from the edges into the centre, then refreeze. After 3 hours fork over again to get a nice flaky effect and serve. If freezing for longer transfer a to a smaller deeper container for easy storage. If frozen hard transfer to the refrigerator for about 30 minutes and fork over again before serving.

GRATTACHECCA

During the hot Roman summers small chioschi *(kiosks) sell* grattachecca – *the Roman name for granita. Scraping big blocks of ice with an iron implement called a* grattuga, *thin shavings are produced, put in cups, covered with flavoured sugar syrups then topped with pieces of iced or fresh fruit and coconut chunks. The most famous of these* chioschi *is Sora Mirella on the Ponte Cestio in Trastevere – it has been there since 1905. These were the only oases that Rome had before the gelaterias opened on almost every street corner.*

10 ice cubes per serving

Sciroppa di Lamponi
Raspberry Syrup
Makes 225 ml/8 fl oz/1 cup

250 g/9 oz/generous 2 cups
   raspberries
400 g/14 oz/2 cups sugar
125 ml/4 fl oz/$^1/_2$ cup water
Juice of 1 lemon
2 tbsp rosewater

Sciroppa di Arancia
Orange Syrup
Makes 225 ml/8 fl oz/1 cup

200 g/7 oz/1 cup sugar
400 ml/14 fl oz/1$^3/_4$ cups
   freshly squeezed orange
   juice, about 4 large oranges
Thin rind from one of the
   oranges (without pith)
Juice of 1 lemon
2 tbsp rosewater

For one glass crush 10 ice cubes in an ice crusher. If you prefer a finer texture, break the cubes up a little, put in a food processor and crush to the desired effect. Pour over the syrup and eat with a spoon.

To make the raspberry syrup, put the raspberries, sugar and water in a wide saucepan and dissolve the sugar over a low heat. Increase the heat and bring to the boil, then simmer rapidly for 5 minutes. Add the lemon juice and simmer for a further 8 minutes until the temperature is almost 100°C/212°F, or when the spoon leaves a parting when pulled across the bottom of the pan. Stir occasionally with a wooden spoon to prevent sticking. Put a metal sieve (strainer) over a bowl and push the syrup through with the back of a ladle. Add the rosewater and pour into a bottle or jar, then cool and chill until ready to use.

To make the orange syrup, put the sugar, juice and rind in a wide saucepan and heat gently to dissolve the sugar. Increase the heat and bring to the boil, then simmer rapidly for 5 minutes. Add the lemon juice and simmer for a further 8 minutes until the temperature is almost 105°C/221°F, or the spoon leaves a parting when pulled across the bottom of the pan. Stir occasionally with a wooden spoon to prevent sticking. Put a metal sieve over a bowl and push the syrup through with the back of a ladle. Add the rosewater and pour into a bottle or jar, then cool and chill until ready to use.

Both syrups will keep in the refrigerator for up to two days. If they are too gelatinous to pour (yes, they are that gloopy!) add a tablespoon of water or rosewater to loosen them slightly.

SORBETTE

Pear Sorbetto

SORBETTO DI PERE

Cooked pears are used in so many Italian desserts, but for me this is the most delicious way to use them (illustrated on p.43). There are different varieties available in Italy almost throughout the year. I like to put a little grappa in the mixture – it adds a superb flavour. This digestive liqueur is distilled from grape skins and pips – in fact the leftovers from wine making.

Serves 6

200 ml/7 fl oz/scant 1 cup
   pure organic apple juice
1 kg/2 lb 4 oz pears, such
   as Abate Fetel or a similar
   variety
Juice of 2 lemons
150 g/5 oz/scant $\frac{1}{2}$ cup acacia
   honey
2 tbsp grappa
Pear crisps, to serve (p.148)

Pour the apple juice into a saucepan. Peel and core the pears and slice into the juice. Add the lemon and honey and cook the pears over a medium heat for about 8 minutes, or until very tender.

Strain through a sieve (strainer) set over a bowl. Put the pear pieces collected in the sieve into a blender and process to a purée. If necessary, add a little of the liquid from the bowl. Mix the purée into the juices in the bowl and leave to chill in the refrigerator.

Churn using an ice cream machine following the manufacturer's instructions until frozen, or still freeze using the method on p.19. Transfer to a freezerproof container, cover and freeze for 1 hour.

If it is frozen for longer and becomes too hard, remove lid and transfer to the refrigerator for about 15 minutes to soften before serving.

"Flower" of Orange Sorbetto

SORBETTO DI FIOR D'ARANCIA

Fragrant and refreshing this sorbetto can be used scooped into a breakfast brioche or into frozen orange shells – save 8 half orange shells and freeze if making this for the Conchiglia d'Arancia con Meringa *(Orange Shell with Meringue) recipe on p.144. Take time to find a good quality orange flower water.*

Serves 6–8

150 g/5 oz/³/₄ cup caster
    (superfine) sugar
50 g/2 oz glucose (dextrose)
    powder
200 ml/7 fl oz/scant 1 cup
    water
4 tbsp orange flower water
16 oranges

Put the sugar, glucose (dextrose) powder and water in a saucepan and heat gently to allow the sugar to dissolve, about 4 minutes. Swirl the liquid around the pan to dislodge any sugar crystals still on the bottom, then transfer to a bowl to cool. Add the orange flower water and leave to chill in the refrigerator until required.

Meanwhile, squeeze the oranges and put the juice and the bits caught in the squeezer through a sieve (strainer) set over a bowl. Add the sieved juice to the syrup.

Churn using an ice cream machine following the manufacturer's instructions until frozen, or still freeze using the method on p.19. Transfer to a freezerproof container, cover and freeze for 2 hours.

If it is frozen for longer and becomes too hard, remove lid and transfer to the refrigerator for about 10 minutes to soften before serving.

SORBETTO DI CIOCCOLATO AL PEPERONCINO

This has a lovely subtle chilli hit. You can play around with this recipe, as there are so many wonderfully flavoured chocolates out there at the moment all waiting to be experimented with. The artisan gelato-makers who are dedicated to marrying just the right flavours use the best chocolate available.

Serves 4–6

125 g/4^1/$_2$ oz chilli-flavoured
   plain dark (bittersweet)
   chocolate
75 g/3 oz plain dark (bittersweet) chocolate (plus a little
   extra to serve (optional))
450 ml/15^1/$_2$ fl oz/scant 2 cups
   cold water
100 g/4 oz/^{1}/$_2$ cup caster
   (superfine) sugar
cones and sugar sprinkles, to
   serve (optional)

Break the chocolate into a saucepan and add 350 ml/12 fl oz/1^1/$_2$ cups of the water. Melt the chocolate over a low heat, then stir well and add the sugar. Heat gently to dissolve the sugar. Increase the heat a little to allow the mixture to bubble gently for 10 minutes. Stir occasionally to ensure that it does not stick to the bottom of the pan.

When the mixture is syrupy pour into a bowl, then place in a larger bowl of cold water and leave to stand for 25 minutes. Whisk in the remaining 100 ml/3^1/$_2$ fl oz/generous ^{1}/$_3$ cup of cold water and chill in the refrigerator for 15 minutes.

Churn in an ice cream machine following the manufacturer's instructions until frozen, or still freeze following the method on p.19. Transfer to a freezerproof container, cover and freeze for 1 hour before serving.

If it is frozen for longer and becomes too hard, remove lid and transfer to the refrigerator for 15 minutes to soften before serving.

Serve in cones dippped first into melted chocolate, then into sugar sprinkles.

Raspberry Sorbetto

SORBETTO DI LAMPONI

This is my favourite sorbetto scooped into a large size cone already loaded with scoops of orange, lemon and lychee (litchi) to take on my passeggiata *– my evening stroll around town, true Italian style. In season, the array of white and red raspberries in the Campo Di Fiori market in Rome is very special. If you can get them, use white raspberries in this recipe – they are actually a pinky peach colour, not white at all – and serve together with a batch of red.*

Serves 4–6

250 g/9 oz raspberries
25 g/1 oz glucose (dextrose)
    powder
225 ml/8 fl oz/1 cup water
Juice of 1 lemon
125 g/4$^{1}/_{2}$ oz/$^{2}/_{3}$ cup caster
    (superfine) sugar

Put the raspberries and glucose (dextrose) powder in a blender with the lemon juice and set aside.

Put the sugar and water in a saucepan and heat gently to allow the sugar to dissolve, about 4 minutes. Swirl the liquid around the pan to dislodge any sugar crystals still on the bottom, then remove from the heat and leave to cool for 20 minutes.

Pour the cooled sugar syrup over the raspberries in the blender and process to a purée. Pour into a nylon sieve (strainer) set over a bowl and push the solids through in a circular motion with the back of a ladle. Discard the pips left behind. Leave the mixture to chill in the refrigerator for 30 minutes.

Churn using an ice cream machine following the manufacturer's instructions until frozen, or still freeze following the method on p.19. Transfer to a freezerproof container, cover and freeze for 4 hours.

If it is frozen for longer and becomes too hard, remove lid and transfer to the refrigerator 15 minutes before serving to soften.

Red Rose Sorbetto

SORBETTO DI ROSA ROSSA

Make sure your scented rose blooms are from a source that does not use chemical sprays. One of the many uses of glycerine is to preserve flowers, and here it works its alchemy to transform the unpromising murky colour of the steeped petals into something special. As a child I would make perfumed potions from rose petals and would always be disappointed with the colour until my mother showed me this trick.

Serves 4–6

250 g/9 oz/1¼ cups caster
   (superfine) sugar

450 ml/15 fl oz/scant 2 cups
   cold water

100 g/4 oz heavily scented red
   rose petals, about 16 roses,
   plus extra petals for
   crystallizing, or use the
   ready-made sort

6 tbsp rose essence (rosewater)

2 tsp glycerine

Juice of 1 lemon

For crystallizing

1 egg white, lightly whisked

100 g/4 oz/½ cup caster
   (superfine) sugar

Put the sugar and 250 ml/8 fl oz/1 cup of the water in a saucepan and heat gently to allow the sugar to dissolve, about 4 minutes. Put the rose petals into the sugar syrup just to wilt them slightly, then add 200 ml/7 fl oz/scant 1 cup cold water and the rose essence and leave to cool for 30 minutes. When cooled add the glycerine.

Leave the petals to steep for 5 hours, or overnight, giving the petals the occasional squeeze.

Add the lemon juice and pour the mixture through a sieve (strainer) set over a bowl. Churn using an ice cream machine following the manufacturer's instructions until frozen, or still freeze following the method on p.19. Transfer to a freezerproof container, cover and freeze for 4 hours before serving.

If it is frozen for longer and becomes too hard, remove lid and transfer to the refrigerator 20–30 minutes before serving to soften.

To make the crystallized petals, paint the extra rose petals with egg white and dip into the caster (superfine) sugar. Lay them on a wire rack in a warm, dry place until crunchy, then store in an airtight container for up to a week.

Blackberry Sorbetto

SORBETTO DI MORA

This wonderfully dark sorbetto has such an intense flavour. Mora is also the name given to the ancient mulberry fruit – difficult to obtain unless blessed with a tree of your own. Use fresh blackberries preferably, but if you have frozen, use them just 20 minutes after taking them from the freezer.

Serves 6

125 g/4 1/2 oz/scant 2/3 cup
  caster (superfine) sugar
225 ml/8 fl oz/1 cup water
250 g/9 oz/1 3/4 cups
  blackberries
25 g/1 oz glucose (dextrose)
  powder
Juice of 1 lime

Put the sugar and water in a saucepan and heat gently to allow the sugar to dissolve, about 4 minutes. Swirl the liquid around the pan to dislodge any sugar crystals still on the bottom, then transfer to a bowl to cool.

Put the blackberries and glucose (dextrose) powder in a blender with the cooled syrup and lime juice and process to a purée. Pour the purée into a sieve (strainer) set over a bowl and push the solids through in a circular motion with the back of a ladle. Discard what is left behind in the sieve. Leave the mixture to chill in the refrigerator for 30 minutes.

Churn using an ice cream machine following the manufacturer's instructions until frozen, or still freeze using the method on p.19. Transfer to a freezerproof container, cover and freeze for 1 hour.

If it is frozen for longer and becomes hard, remove lid and transfer to the refrigerator to soften 20 minutes before serving.

Elderflower Sorbetto

FIORI DI SAMBUCO

Good quality cordial is a must for this recipe, making it the easiest and the most satisfying sorbetto to make. If you produce your own cordial do ensure the flowerheads are picked in the morning before the sun gets to them and from a position that is unpolluted by vehicle fumes. This sorbetto is very pretty served in shot glasses and presented, buried in ice, in a large flowered iced bowl (p.150) for a special dinner along with other flavours of sorbetto, such as Sorbetto di Rosa Rossa *(p.51).*

Serves 4–6

400 ml/14 fl oz/1¾ cups
  elderflower cordial (see
  Suppliers p.159)
150 ml/5 fl oz/⅔ cup spring
  water

Mix the cordial and water together in a bowl and chill in the freezer for 10 minutes.

Churn using an ice cream machine following the manufacturer's instructions until frozen, or still freeze using the method on p.19. Transfer to a freezerproof container, cover and freeze for 3 hours.

If it is frozen for longer and becomes hard, remove lid and transfer to the refrigerator to soften 25–30 minutes before serving.

Mango Sorbetto

SORBETTO DI MANGO

Serves 6

100 g/4 oz/½ cup caster
  (superfine) sugar
100 g/4 oz glucose (dextrose)
  powder
100 ml/3½ fl oz/generous
  ⅓ cup water
500 g/1 lb 2 oz canned mango
  pulp

Put the sugar, glucose (dextrose) powder and water in a saucepan and heat gently to allow the sugar to dissolve, about 4 minutes. Swirl the liquid around the pan to dislodge any sugar crystals still on the bottom, then transfer to a bowl to cool.

Add the mango pulp to the cooled syrup and leave to chill for 30 minutes. Churn using an ice cream machine following the manufacturer's instructions until frozen, or still freeze using the method on p.19. Transfer to a freezerproof container, cover and freeze for 4 hours.

This sorbetto remains quite soft, even if it is frozen for longer.

Cactus Pear Sorbetto

SORBETTO DI FICO D'INDIA

Prickly cactus pears were brought from the Americas around the 16th century and now grow profusely, both wild and cultivated, around the Mediterranean. The prickles are removed mechanically so don't be put off making this dessert. Cactus pears are an amazing delicacy and come in a range of shades from gold to yellowy green, purple, pink and red, all with shockingly bright-coloured flesh.

Serves 4–6

100 g/4 oz/$\frac{1}{2}$ cup caster
   (superfine) sugar

25 g/1 oz glucose (dextrose)
   powder

250 ml/9 fl oz/generous 1 cup
   water

Juice of 2 lemons

15 cactus pears, about 1 kg/
   2$\frac{1}{4}$ lb in weight

$\frac{1}{4}$ of a batch of *Meringa
   Italiana* (p.153)

Put the sugar, glucose (dextrose) powder and water in a saucepan and heat gently to allow the sugar to dissolve, about 4 minutes. Swirl the liquid around the pan to dislodge any sugar crystals still on the bottom, then add the lemon juice and transfer to a bowl to cool.

Meanwhile, peel the cactus pears by sticking a fork into the side and cutting off each end with a sharp knife. Slice off the thin skin using the knife and fork to avoid any tiny prickles that may be left behind. As each one is peeled put it into a blender. Purée in 2 batches, pouring each batch into a nylon sieve (strainer) set over a bowl. Push the solids through in a circular motion with the back of a ladle. Mix the cooled sugar syrup into the purée then add a little to the *Meringa* mixture, whisking well to mix before adding the remainder. Leave to chill in the refrigerator for 30 minutes.

Churn using an ice cream machine following the manufacturer's instructions until frozen, or still freeze using the method on p.19. Transfer to a freezerproof container, cover and freeze for 2 hours before serving.

If it is frozen for longer and becomes too hard, remove lid and transfer to the refrigerator to soften 45 minutes before serving.

Tip: Make a full batch of the *Meringa Italia* and use the rest to make some meringues – pipe onto baking (cookie) trays and cook them at 120°C/250°F/Gas Mark $\frac{3}{4}$ for 1$\frac{1}{2}$ hours. Store in a container for up to 1 week.

White Wine Sorbetto

SORBETTO DI VERNACCIA DI SAN GIMIGNANO

Sergio Dondole of Gelateria d'Piazza in the Tuscan medieval hilltop town of San Gimignano uses the local Vernaccia di San Gimignano wine for this recipe. This wine was considered Italy's finest as far back as Renaissance times and was the first Italian wine to be awarded DOC status, in the mid-'60s. It is rich yet crisp with a heady bouquet, perfect for making my favourite sorbetto. Sergio tells me it should always be served with another flavour and I find kiwi gelato and raspberry sorbetto just right. However, secretly I prefer it on its own!

Serves 6–8

150 g/5 oz/³⁄₄ cup caster (superfine) sugar
175 ml/6 fl oz (³⁄₄ cup) water
400 ml/14 fl oz/1³⁄₄ cups Vernaccia di San Gimignano white wine

Put the sugar and water in a saucepan and heat gently to allow the sugar to dissolve, about 4 minutes. Swirl the liquid around the pan to dislodge any sugar crystals still on the bottom, then transfer to a bowl to cool. Add the wine and stir. Chill in the refrigerator for 30 minutes.

Churn using an ice cream machine following the manufacturer's instructions until frozen, or still freeze using the method on p.19. Transfer to a freezerproof container, cover and freeze for 2–4 hours before serving.

Don't worry that this sorbetto remains very soft – this is due to the amount of wine used. I prefer it this way because if more water was added (which would freeze it harder) it would dilute the flavour.

If it is frozen for longer, the wine syrup may separate a little. Simply transfer to a cold bowl, whisk with electric beaters and re-freeze for 1 hour before serving.

Right: *Sorbetto di Vernacchia di San Gimignano* (right of picture) shown with *Gelato di Kiwi* (p.117).

Lemon Sorbetto in Brioche

SORBETTO DI LIMONE TRA BRIOCHE

There are about ten varieties of lemons in Sicily, such as the Feminello, *the variety the Arabs brought to the island in the 9th century. My* Sorbetto di Limone *is a little sharper than most as I use more lemons, but I prefer it. The Sicilians love this sorbetto even above the coffee granita for breakfast, scooped and stuffed into a brioche for a zingy start to the day. Young Italians also like a scoop added to their beer.*

Serves 4–6

Grated rind and juice of
  16 unwaxed lemons (about
  600 ml/1 pint/2$\frac{1}{2}$ cups)
300 g/10 oz/1$\frac{1}{2}$ cups caster
  (superfine) sugar
500 ml/16 fl oz/2 cups cold
  water
Mini brioche, to serve

Put the lemon rind, sugar and the water into a saucepan and heat gently to allow the sugar to dissolve, about 4 minutes. Swirl the liquid around the pan to dislodge any sugar crystals still on the bottom, then transfer to a bowl to cool.

Strain the mixture through a sieve (strainer) set over a bowl and add the squeezed lemon juice. Discard the contents of the sieve.

Churn using an ice cream machine following the manufacturer's instructions until frozen, or still freeze using the method on p.19. Transfer to a freezerproof container, cover and freeze for 3 hours before serving.

If it is frozen for longer and becomes hard, remove lid and transfer to the refrigerator to soften 15 minutes before serving.

Strawberry Sorbetto

SORBETTO DI FRAGOLE

Packed full of flavour when the strawberries are ripe and red – summer is the best time for this sorbetto. Serve with some other flavours scooped into little bowls or swirl into the Gelato di Fragole *(p.80). If you want an even brighter red colour, add a little grenadine to the syrup – choose a non-alcoholic brand.*

Serves 4–6

500 g/1 lb 2 oz ripe red
  strawberries
25 g/1 oz glucose (dextrose)
  powder
100 g/4 oz/^{1}/$_2$ cup caster
  (superfine) sugar
100 ml/3^1/$_2$ fl oz/ generous
  ^{1}/$_3$ cup water
Juice of 1 lime
2 tsp grenadine (optional)

Wash and hull the strawberries, put in a blender with the glucose (dextrose) powder and process to a purée. Pour into a nylon sieve (strainer) set over a bowl and push the purée through in a circular motion with the back of a ladle. Discard the pulp left behind in the sieve. Leave to chill in the refrigerator until needed.

Put the sugar and water in a saucepan and heat gently to dissolve the sugar, about 4 minutes. Swirl the liquid around the pan to dislodge any sugar crystals still on the bottom, then transfer to a bowl to cool.

Mix the strawberry purée and sugar syrup together, add the lime juice and the grenadine, if using. Churn using an ice cream machine following the manufacturer's instructions until frozen, or still freeze following the method on p.19. Transfer to a freezerproof container, cover and freeze for 3 hours before serving.

If it is frozen for longer and becomes hard, remove lid and transfer to the refrigerator to soften 20–30 minutes before serving.

Overleaf: The breathtaking view out
from the walls of San Gimignano.

SORBETTO BELLINI

This is the classic Venetian Harry's Bar cocktail – named after the Venetian artist Giovanni Bellini – turned into an equally glamorous sorbetto. I cook the peaches to intensify the flavour and it also helps to maintain the rich colour that turns a magnificent rosy hue when teamed with raspberries.

Serves 4–6

6 peaches

100 g/4 oz/scant 1 cup raspberries

25 g/1 oz glucose (dextrose) powder

100 g/4 oz/½ cup caster (superfine) sugar

1 bottle Prosecco Di Valdobbiadene or other good quality Prosecco, chilled

Preheat the oven to 200°C/400°F/Gas Mark 6. Cut the peaches in half, but leave the stones (pits) in. Arrange the peach halves on a baking (cookie) sheet and dust with 2 tablespoons of the sugar. Cover with foil and bake for 20–30 minutes until tender. Remove from the oven and leave to cool before peeling off the skins and removing the stones.

Put the peach flesh into a blender with the raspberries and glucose (dextrose) powder and process to a purée. Tip the mixture into a nylon sieve (strainer) set over a bowl and push the purée through in a circular motion with the back of a ladle. Discard anything that remains in the sieve. Leave to chill for 30 minutes.

Put the remaining sugar into a saucepan with 200 ml/7 fl oz/ scant 1 cup of the Prosecco and heat gently to allow the sugar to dissolve, about 4 minutes. Swirl the liquid around the pan to dislodge any sugar crystals still on the bottom, then remove from the heat and leave to cool. Mix into the fruit purée.

Freeze in an ice cream maker following the manufacturer's instructions until frozen. If wished you can serve the mixture when it is soft and floppy straight from the machine or put it in a freezerproof container, cover and transfer it to the freezer for 1 hour. Alternatively, still freeze following the method on p.19. If it is frozen for longer and freezes hard, remove lid and transfer to the refrigerator 20 minutes before serving to soften.

To serve, put a few miniature scoops of sorbetto into a wide-bowled champagne glass and top with the chilled Prosecco.

Apple Sorbetto

SORBETTO DI MELE

Although technically a gelato, as sorbetti aren't usually made with dairy products, the very small quantity of cream in this recipe means it retains a sorbetto texture. I like this served with the Apple Crisps on p.148 made into a tremezzino *– a sandwich.*

Serves 6–8

650 g/1 lb 7 oz good-flavoured
  apples such as Cox,
  quartered and cored
  (skins on)
125 g/4¹/₂ oz/scant ²/₃ cup
  caster (superfine) sugar
50 g/2 oz glucose (dextrose)
  powder
200 ml/7 fl oz/scant 1 cup
  water
200 ml/7 fl oz/scant 1 cup
  apple juice
100 ml/3¹/₂ fl oz/generous
  ¹/₃ cup whipping cream
3 tbsp Vin Santo (La Sala
  is good)
Apple Crisps, to serve (p.148)

Roughly slice the apples into a large saucepan and add the sugar, glucose (dextrose) powder, water and juice. Heat gently until the sugar has dissolved, then increase the heat and bring to the boil. Reduce the heat and simmer for 10 minutes or until the apples are very soft. Remove from the heat and leave to cool for 10 minutes.

Process the cooled mixture in a blender until a purée forms, then pour into a nylon sieve (strainer) set over a bowl and push the purée through in a circular motion with the back of a ladle. Leave to cool for 1 hour then mix in the whipping cream and Vin Santo. Chill in the refrigerator for 30 minutes.

Churn using an ice cream machine following the manufacturer's instructions until frozen, or still freeze using the method on p.19. Transfer to a freezerproof container, cover and freeze for 1¹/₂ hours before serving.

If it is frozen for longer and becomes hard, remove lid and transfer to the refrigerator to soften 20 minutes before serving.

To serve, layer the sorbetto with Apple Crisps to make a *tremezzino* (sandwich).

SORBETTO DI AVOCADO

I like this sorbetto made only by the still freezing method detailed below because it seems to temper the texture and flavour much more sympathetically than a rapid freeze. It is delicious served dowsed in Italian Saba *– a cooked and concentrated grape juice dating back to the Roman Empire. It also makes a lovely appetizer for a summer garden lunch served with long, knobbly Italian breadsticks.*

Serves 6

60 g/2½ oz/scant ⅓ cup caster (superfine) sugar

200 ml/7 fl oz/scant 1 cup water

Pinch of salt

Juice of 2 lemons

125 ml/4 fl oz/½ cup sour cream

3 small ripe avocados

Put the sugar, 100 ml/3½ fl oz/generous ⅓ cup of the water and salt in a saucepan and heat gently to allow the sugar to dissolve, about 4 minutes. Swirl the liquid around the pan to dislodge any sugar crystals still on the bottom, then transfer to a bowl to cool. Leave to chill in the refrigerator for 30 minutes.

Pour the lemon juice into a blender and add the sour cream. Cut the avocados in half and remove the stone (pit). Using a teaspoon, scoop the flesh from each half straight into the blender and process to a purée. Transfer the mixture to a freezerproof container. Pour the remaining 100 ml/3½ fl oz/generous ⅓ cup of water into the blender and process briefly, then pour into the mixture in the freezerproof container and mix well.

Freeze for 1½ hours, then remove from the freezer and fork over the mixture to bring the frozen edges into the centre. Return to the freezer and freeze for a further 1 hour. Remove from the freezer and mix again with a fork. Return to the freezer for another 1½ hours.

Transfer the mixture to a food processor and process until smooth, then transfer to a freezerproof container, cover, and re-freeze for 1 hour. The texture is just right to serve now but if it is frozen for longer and becomes too hard, transfer to the refrigerator to soften 45 minutes before serving.

Lychee Sorbetto

SORBETTO DI LYCHEE

This is the cheat's way using canned lychees (litchis), but they are still very good, full of flavour and come without stones! The texture of the sorbetto is quite snow-like. I like it served in shot glasses with Gelato di Liquirizia *(p.92).*

Serves 4–6

125 g/4^1/$_2$ oz/^{5}/$_8$ cup caster (superfine) sugar

100 ml/3^1/$_2$ fl oz/generous ^{1}/$_3$ cup water

3 x 425 g/15 oz cans lychees (litchis) in a light syrup

Juice of ^{1}/$_2$ lemon

Put the sugar and water in a saucepan and heat gently to dissolve the sugar, about 4 minutes. Swirl the liquid around the pan to dislodge any sugar crystals still on the bottom, then transfer to a bowl to cool.

Drain the lychees (litchis), put them into a blender and process to a purée. Pour the purée into a sieve (strainer) set over a bowl and push the purée through with the back of a ladle using a circular motion. Discard the pulp left behind in the sieve. Chill in the refrigerator.

Pour the syrup into the lychee juice and add the lemon juice. Churn using an ice cream machine following the manufacturer's instructions until frozen, or still freeze following the method on p.19. Transfer to a freezerproof container, cover and freeze for 3 hours before serving.

If it is frozen for longer and becomes too hard, remove lid and transfer to the refrigerator to soften 30 minutes before serving.

SORBETTO DI FRUTTA DI PASSIONE

I prefer the intense flavour so many passion fruit give to this recipe, but try it with fewer if you wish. Use fruits with wrinkled skin – this way you know they are fully ripe and beautifully scented.

Serves 4–6

150 g/5 oz/³/4 cup caster
   (superfine) sugar
150 ml/5 fl oz/²/3 cup water
Juice of 2 lemons
12 passion fruit

Put the sugar and water into a saucepan and heat gently to allow the sugar to dissolve, about 4 minutes. Swirl the liquid around the pan to dislodge any sugar crystals still on the bottom, then transfer to a bowl to cool.

Cut the passion fruit in half and scoop the flesh out with a teaspoon into a blender. Process briefly then pour into a nylon sieve (strainer) set over a bowl. This just separates the seeds from their jelly-like casing without pulverizing them. Push as much flesh and juice through as possible in a circular motion with the back of a ladle. Mix the sugar syrup and lemon juice into the bowl. Chill in the refrigerator for 30 minutes.

Churn using an ice cream machine following the manufacturer's instructions until frozen, or still freeze using the method on p.19. Transfer to a freezerproof container, cover and freeze for 1¹/2 hours before serving.

If it is frozen for longer and becomes hard, remove lid and transfer to the refrigerator to soften 15 minutes before serving.

Pomegranate Sorbetto

SORBETTO DI MELAGRANA

Originating in Persia, the pomegranate was, until recently, most popular around the Middle East and Mediterranean. It has since rapidly gained recognition as a health-giving superfruit. It is worth taking time to prepare this fine-flavoured fruit with its glassy, juice-laden seeds. Use a lemon squeezer or an electric juicer to extract the juice.

Serves 4–6

125 g/4$\frac{1}{2}$ oz/scant $\frac{2}{3}$ cup
   caster (superfine) sugar
100 ml/3$\frac{1}{2}$ fl oz/generous
   $\frac{1}{3}$ cup water
Juice of 1 lemon
6 large pomegranates (to give
   600 ml/1 pint/2$\frac{1}{2}$ cups
   of juice)

To serve
Crushed pomegranate ice
   cubes
Sete al Liquore (macerated
   pomegranate seeds), see
   p.152

Put the sugar and water in a saucepan and heat gently to allow the sugar to dissolve, about 4 minutes. Swirl the liquid around the pan to dislodge any sugar crystals still on the bottom, then add the lemon juice and transfer to a bowl to cool.

Half the pomegranates one at a time to avoid losing any juice and, using a lemon squeezer or an electric juicer, extract as much juice as possible. It is often tricky to get every last bit of juice as the juicy seeds are tightly packed within their skin, so it's best to give a final squeeze by hand. Pass the juice through a nylon sieve (strainer) set over a bowl to catch any bits then mix into the cooled sugar syrup.

Churn using an ice cream machine following the manufacturer's instructions until frozen, or still freeze using the method on p.19. Transfer to a freezerproof container, cover and freeze for 1 hour before serving.

If it is frozen for longer and becomes hard, remove lid and transfer to the refrigerator to soften 40 minutes before serving.

Serve with crushed pomegranate ice cubes (simply pour the juice directly into an ice tray and freeze) and a spoonful of *Sete al Liquore* (macerated pomegranate seeds).

Pesto Sorbetto

SORBETTO DI PESTO ALLA GENOVESE

This can be served as part of an antipasti with Italian breadsticks for dipping. Ideally use salty-tasting San Pellegrino for the water in this recipe.

Put the sugar and 60 ml/2 fl oz/$^1/_4$ cup of the sparkling water in a saucepan and heat gently to allow the sugar to dissolve, about 4 minutes. Swirl the liquid around the pan to dislodge any sugar crystals still on the bottom, then transfer to a bowl to cool.

Put the syrup, basil, garlic, pine nuts and Parmesan into a blender and process until a purée forms. With the motor running, add the oil in a steady stream, followed by the remaining sparkling water.

Churn using an ice cream machine following the manufacturer's instructions until frozen, or still freeze using the method on p.19. Transfer to a freezerproof container, cover and freeze for 1 hour before serving.

If it is frozen for longer and becomes hard, remove lid and transfer to the refrigerator to soften 30 minutes before serving.

Serves 6–8

60 g/2$^1/_2$ oz/scant $^1/_3$ cup caster
   (superfine) sugar
310 ml/10 fl oz/scant 1$^1/_4$ cups
   sparkling water (ideally San
   Pellegrino), chilled
75 g/3 oz fresh basil leaves
1 small garlic clove blanched
   in boiling water for 5 minutes, peeled and crushed
3 tbsp pine nuts, lightly toasted
40 g/1$^1/_2$ oz Parmesan cheese,
   finely grated
5 tbsp extra virgin olive oil

Fennel Sorbetto

SORBETTO DI FINOCCHIO

I made this after being given a little bottle of Liquore di Finocchietto, *a wild fennel liqueur from Sorrento. Use some of the fennel herb as well if you grow it as this adds more colour to the sorbetto. The blanching and puréeing of the fennel is left to the last second before freezing so that all the colour and flavour are retained. This is another sorbetto I prefer to make by the still freezing method.*

Serves 6

175 g/6 oz/scant 1 cup caster
　(superfine) sugar
150 ml/5 fl oz/²/₃ cup water
100 ml/3¹/₂ fl oz/generous
　¹/₃ cup dry white wine
Pinch of salt
500 g/1 lb 2 oz fresh Florence
　fennel bulb with green
　fronds
2 fresh fennel herb sprigs
2 tbsp *Liquore di Finocchietto*
　(optional)

Put the sugar, water, wine and salt in a saucepan and heat gently to allow the sugar to dissolve, about 4 minutes. Swirl the liquid around the pan to dislodge any sugar crystals still on the bottom, then transfer to a bowl to cool. Chill in the refrigerator for 30 minutes.

Wash and trim the base from the fennel bulb, then put the green fronds in a nylon sieve (strainer) set in the sink and snip in the extra fennel herb sprigs. Thinly slice the fennel bulb and blanch in a saucepan of boiling water for 1 minute. Immediately pour the contents of the pan over the fennel fronds in the sieve and refresh under cold running water until completely cold. This ensures that the bright colour is retained and also stops the fennel from cooking any further.

Transfer it to a blender together with a little of the chilled sugar syrup and process until a purée forms. Pour the mixture into a nylon sieve (strainer) set over a bowl and push as much of the solids through as possible in a circular motion with the back of a ladle. Transfer the mixture left in the sieve to the blender together with the remaining chilled sugar syrup and process to a purée. Pour the mixture back into the sieve and push as much solid material through as possible.

Mix in the *liquore* (if using), transfer to a freezerproof container and still freeze using the method on p.19. Cover and freeze for 2 hours before serving.

If it is frozen for longer and becomes hard, remove lid and transfer to the refrigerator to soften 40 minutes before serving.

GHIACCIOLO ALLA FRUTTA

These are true water ices – no churning involved, just pure natural juices sweetened to your personal taste and frozen with wooden lolly (popsicle) sticks for easy eating. Just for fun, dip into some rich melted dark chocolate and colourful Hundreds and Thousands (sprinkles) – something I loved to do when my children were small for the occasional treat.

Makes 12,
   4 of each flavour

Orange Lollies

Juice of 2 medium oranges

$1^{1}/_{2}$ tsp caster (superfine) sugar

Pomegranate Lollies

Juice of 4 large pomegranates

1 tsp caster (superfine) sugar

Raspberry Lollies

100 g/4 oz/$^{1}/_{2}$ cup raspberries

100 ml/$3^{1}/_{2}$ fl oz/generous
   $^{1}/_{3}$ cup spring water

Squeeze of lemon juice

2 tsp caster (superfine) sugar

To decorate

125 g/$4^{1}/_{2}$ oz/scant $^{2}/_{3}$ cup plain
   (bittersweet) chocolate

30 g/1 oz Hundreds and
   Thousands (sprinkles)

To make the orange lollies, put the orange juice in a bowl and mix the sugar into the juice.

To make the pomegranate lollies, put the pomegranate juice into a separate bowl and mix the sugar into the juice.

To make the raspberry lollies, put the raspberries, water, lemon juice and sugar into a blender and purée. Pour into a nylon sieve (strainer) set over a bowl, push gently to get the juices flowing through and discard what is left behind. Add extra water if necessary.

Pour each mixture into 4 x 50 ml/2 fl oz ice lolly (popsicle) moulds, cover with tin foil and insert a wooden lolly stick into the centre of each. Freeze for 6 hours or overnight.

Un-mould the lollies by running the moulds briefly under a warm running tap to loosen, put them on a wax paper-lined tray and re-freeze.

Melt the chocolate in a small bowl, and leave to cool for about 15 minutes, so it's still runny. Put the Hundreds and Thousands (sprinkles) in a cup. Dip each lolly into the chocolate, let any excess drip off and then dip into the Hundreds and Thousands to coat the tips. Put back in the freezer until ready to eat (best eaten right away but no longer than overnight).

GELATI

Custard Gelato

GELATO DI CREMA

This is one of the basic gelati, and is perfect for using in layered desserts like the Neapolitan *(p.141) and dome-shaped moulds, such as* Spumone *(p.135). The Gelateria Combattenti in San Gimignano makes a "spaghetti" gelato out of this.*

Serves 8

Basic mix makes about
1.2 litres/2 pints/5 cups
before churning

300 ml/10 fl oz/1 $\frac{1}{4}$ cups
double (heavy) cream
700 ml/1 $\frac{1}{4}$ pints/3 cups full
cream (whole) milk
8 large egg yolks
200 g/7 oz/1 cup caster
(superfine) sugar
3 tbsp skimmed milk powder

Put the cream and milk in a saucepan and gently heat until bubbles start to appear around the side of the pan.

Meanwhile, whisk the egg yolks, sugar and skimmed milk powder together in a heatproof bowl until pale in colour. Pour in the hot milk mixture and stir well.

Wash out the saucepan and pour the mixture back in. Cook over a medium heat with a heat diffuser mat under the pan, stirring constantly with a wooden spoon, for 8–10 minutes until it reaches 75°C/167°F on a thermometer. Do not boil or let the mixture get any hotter otherwise it will curdle. The custard will thicken a little as it cools. Transfer the mixture to a wide bowl and leave to cool. Chill in the refrigerator for 30 minutes.

Churn using an ice cream machine following the manufacturer's instructions until frozen (you may need to churn in 2 batches), or still freeze following the method on p.19. Transfer to a freezerproof container, cover and freeze for 2 $\frac{1}{2}$ hours before serving. If it is frozen for longer and becomes too hard, remove lid and transfer to the refrigerator to soften about 45 minutes before serving.

Note: You can also add alcohol to this gelato, such as: Amaretto, the most well-known Italian liqueur; Galliano and Strega, the bright yellow herbal liqueurs with strong anise overtones; Frangelico, the hazelnut liqueur; and Sambuca, flavoured with elderberries, anise and other herbs. Because alcohol can inhibit the formation of ice crystals only use about 60 ml/2 fl oz/ $\frac{1}{4}$ cup to every 500 ml/16 fl oz/ 2 cups of unchurned gelato mix, which is about right for liqueurs. Nuts, chocolate and crystallized fruits could be added too, if wished.

GELATO DI FRAGOLE

Choose ripe red strawberries packed full of summer sun for this gelato. Do taste the mixture and add extra lemon juice if you think the flavour needs more of a lift. After churning the gelato, you can make a strawberry swirl. To do this, layer the freshly churned gelato mixture in a freezerproof container with blobs of churned Strawberry Sorbetto (p.59) and swirl with the end of a spoon. Serve with some sliced strawberries.

Serves 6–8

300 ml/10 fl oz/1 ¼ cups full-cream (whole) milk

100 ml/3 ½ fl oz/generous ⅓ cup whipping cream

4 egg yolks

150 g/5 oz/¾ cup caster (superfine) sugar

500 g/1 lb 2 oz ripe strawberries, plus extra to serve

Juice of ½ lemon

Put the milk and cream in a saucepan and gently heat until bubbles start to appear around the side of the pan. Meanwhile, whisk the egg yolks and sugar together in a bowl until pale in colour. Pour in the hot milk mixture and stir well.

Wash out the pan and pour the mixture back in. Cook over a medium heat with a heat diffuser mat under the pan, stirring constantly, for 8–10 minutes. When some of the foam disappears from the surface place a sugar thermometer in the pan and continue to stir until the temperature reads 75°C/167°F. Do not let the mixture get any hotter, otherwise the custard will curdle. The custard will thicken a little as it cools, transfer to a wide bowl and leave to cool.

Hull the strawberries, put them into a blender with the lemon juice and process until a purée forms. Pour into a nylon sieve (strainer) set over a bowl and push the purée through using a circular motion with the back of a ladle. Discard what is left in the sieve. Add the purée to the cold custard. Chill in the refrigerator for 30 minutes.

Churn using an ice cream machine following the manufacturer's instructions until frozen, or still freeze following the method on p.19. Transfer to a freezerproof container, cover and freeze for 4 hours before serving.

If it is frozen for longer and becomes too hard, remove lid and transfer to the refrigerator to soften about 30 minutes before serving.

Lime and Mascarpone Gelato

GELATO DI LIME E MASCARPONE

This is the simplest gelato to make. I particularly like it served with Amarene cherries in syrup. These are the slightly sour cherries – amaro means "sour" – that can be bought in jars. Brand some Italian amaretti morbidi, the small soft almond biscuits, for a few seconds on a hot ridged grill pan to eat with it.

Serves 6–8

200 g/7 oz/1 cup caster
    (superfine) sugar
300 ml/10 fl oz/1$^{1}/_{4}$ cups full
    cream (whole) milk
250 g/9 oz mascarpone
400 g/14 oz limes (makes
    225 ml/8 fl oz/1 cup juice)

Put the sugar and milk in a saucepan and heat gently to allow the sugar to dissolve, about 4 minutes. Swirl the liquid around the pan to dislodge any sugar crystals still on the bottom, then transfer to a bowl to cool.

Put the mascarpone in a bowl and whisk until smooth. Add the cooled milk mixture a little at a time. Squeeze the juice from the limes and add with all the "bits" to the mascarpone mixture. Leave to chill in the refrigerator for 30 minutes.

Churn using an ice cream machine following the manufacturer's instructions until frozen, or still freeze following the method on p.19. Transfer to a freezerproof container, cover and freeze for 3 hours before serving.

If it is frozen for longer and becomes too hard, remove lid and transfer to the refrigerator to soften about 20 minutes before serving.

Espresso Gelato

GELATO AL CAFFÈ

This gelato is so useful, next in line to Gelato di Crema *and* Fior di Latte, *so I prefer to make it in a large quantity. It makes 1.3 litres/2¼ pints/5½ cups of liquid, so it will need to be churned in 2 batches. I like to serve it as a* tramezzino – *a layer of gelati sandwiched between thin sheets of pale coloured meringue (p.153), topped with* panna montata, *the softly whipped cream the Italians so love to embellish their gelati with.*

Serves 12,
    or makes 6–8 *tramezzino*

80 g/2¾ oz finely ground
    coffee
400 ml/14 fl oz/1¾ cups
    boiling water
8 egg yolks
125 g/4½ oz/scant ⅔ cup soft
    brown sugar
Pinch of salt
500 ml/16 fl oz/2 cups
    whipping cream
500 ml/16 fl oz/2 cups full
    cream (whole) milk
1 tsp good quality vanilla
    extract, such as Madagascan
    Bourbon

To serve
Panna Montata (softly whipped
    cream)
Foglio di Meringa Italiana
    (Sheets of Meringue on
    p.153)

Put the coffee into a cafetière and pour on the boiling water. Leave to stand for 15 minutes before pushing down the plunger as far as it will go. Transfer to a bowl and leave to cool.

Whisk the egg yolks, sugar and salt together in a large heatproof bowl until pale in colour. Pour the cream and milk into a saucepan and heat slowly until just coming to the boil, or until bubbles appear around the edge of the pan. Pour into the egg yolk mixture and stir well.

Wash out the pan and pour the mixture back in. Cook over a medium heat with a heat diffuser mat under the pan, stirring constantly, for 8–10 minutes. When some of the foam disappears from the surface place a sugar thermometer in the pan and continue to stir until the temperature reads 75°C/167°F. Do not let the mixture get any hotter, otherwise the custard will curdle. Add the coffee and vanilla, pour into a bowl to cool, then chill in the refrigerator for 30 minutes.

Churn using an ice cream machine following the manufacturer's instructions until frozen, or still freeze following the method on p.19. Transfer to a freezerproof container, cover and freeze for 1½–2 hours before serving. If it is frozen for longer and becomes too hard, remove lid and transfer to the refrigerator to soften about 40 minutes before serving.

Make 6–8 servings of flat scoops of gelato on individual serving plates and add a dollop of softly whipped cream to the tops. Press the sheets of *meringa* to each side of the towers and serve at once.

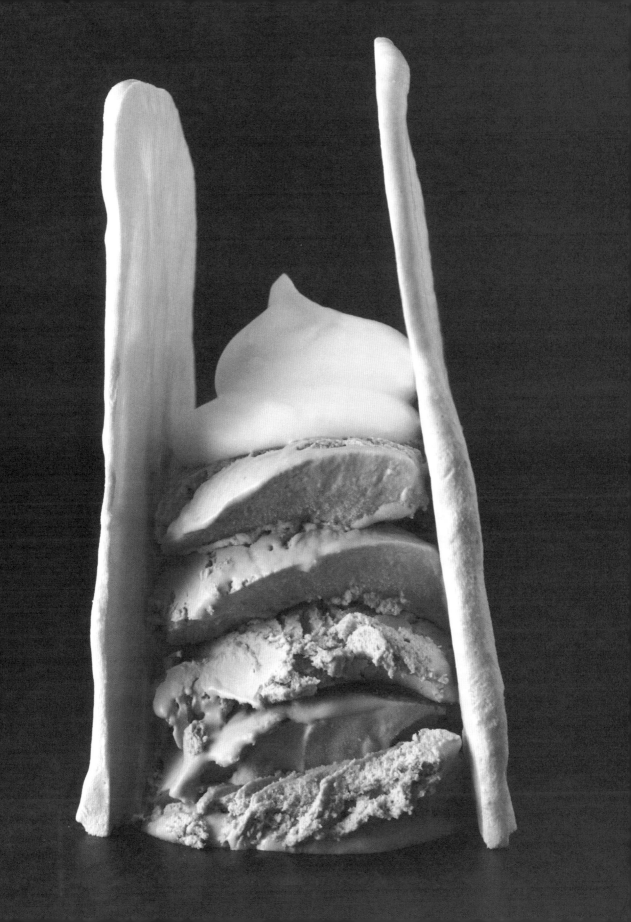

Rice and Mascarpone Gelato

GELATO DI RISO CON MASCARPONE

Do cook the rice well and make sure this gelato is served as soon as it has had the required freezing time, so the rice does not harden completely.

Serves 4–6

4 tbsp skimmed milk powder

850 ml/1 1/2 pints/3 1/2 cups full-
    cream (whole) milk

75 g/3 oz/generous 1/3 cup
    risotto rice

175 g/6 oz/scant 1 cup caster
    (superfine) sugar

6 egg yolks

125 g/4 1/2 oz/scant 2/3 cup
    mascarpone

2 tbsp gin

5 drops orange oil

Whisk the milk powder into 350 ml/12 fl oz/1 1/2 cups of milk in a pan and heat over a medium heat. When bubbles start to appear, add the rice, turn off the heat, cover and leave to soak for 1 hour. Put the pan of rice over a low heat, add 75 g/3 oz/1/3 cup of the sugar and slowly bring to the boil. Put a heat diffuser mat under the pan and continue cooking, stirring occasionally, for a total of 15 minutes. The milk should just make tiny bubbles on the surface. Stir continuously for a further 5 minutes until the rice is sticky.

Put the remaining 500 ml/16 fl oz/2 cups of milk in a pan and gently bring to the boil until bubbles start to appear around the side of the pan. Whisk the egg yolks and the remaining sugar together in a heat-proof bowl until pale in colour. Pour in the hot mixture and stir well. Wash out the pan and pour the mixture back in. Cook over a medium heat with a heat diffuser mat under the pan, stirring constantly, for 8–10 minutes. Place a sugar thermometer in the pan and continue to stir until the temperature reads 75°C/167°F. Do not let the mixture get any hotter, otherwise the custard will curdle. Mix with the rice mixture, cool and chill in the refrigerator for 30 minutes.

Put the mascarpone in a bowl and pour over a little rice custard. Mix well, then add the remainder of the rice custard and mix again. Add the gin and orange oil.

Churn using an ice cream machine following the manufacturer's instructions until frozen. Transfer to a freezerproof container, cover and freeze for 4 hours before serving. Alternatively, strain the custard through a wide mesh sieve (strainer) and still freeze following the method on p.19. After the last processing, put the rice back in, cover and freeze as above. If it is frozen for longer and becomes too hard, remove lid and transfer to the refrigerator to soften 1 3/4 hours before serving.

Rich Chocolate Gelato with Meringues and Hazelnuts

BACIO CON BIANCHINI E NOCCIOLE

Bacio *means "a kiss" and here this ever-popular gelato is untraditionally "kissed" with nutty white meringues and hazelnuts. This is a rich chocolate gelato, which is very popular. I have added the little nutty meringues to add that extra something, as I love these* Bianchini *"little whites" to decorate the top.*

Serves 6–8

350 ml/12 fl oz/1$\frac{1}{2}$ cups full-
  cream (whole) milk
4 eggs
125 g/4$\frac{1}{2}$ oz/$\frac{5}{8}$ cup caster
  (superfine) sugar
250 g/9 oz good quality plain
  dark (bittersweet) chocolate
  with about 54% cocoa
  solids, broken into squares
284 ml/10 fl oz/scant 1$\frac{1}{4}$ cups
  whipping cream
10 Little Meringues (*Bianchini*
  p.149)
3 tbsp skinned and roasted
  hazelnuts, roughly chopped

Pour the milk into a saucepan and heat over a medium heat until bubbles start to appear around the edges.

Meanwhile, whisk the eggs and sugar together in a heatproof bowl. Pour in the hot milk and stir well.

Wash out the pan and pour the mixture back in. Cook over a medium heat with a heat diffuser mat under the pan, stirring constantly, for 8–10 minutes. When some of the foam disappears from the surface place a sugar thermometer in the pan and continue to stir until the temperature reads 75°C/167°F. Do not let the mixture get any hotter, otherwise the custard will curdle.

Add the chocolate squares to the hot custard and stir until melted then leave to cool, and chill in the refrigerator for 30 minutes.

Whip the cream in another bowl until soft peaks form and fold into the chilled chocolate custard.

Churn using an ice cream machine following the manufacturer's instructions until frozen, or still freeze following the method on p.19. Fold in 6 roughly crushed meringues (*bianchini*) and the hazelnuts. Transfer to a freezerproof container, cover and freeze for 2 hours before serving.

If it is frozen for longer and becomes too hard, remove lid and transfer to the refrigerator to soften about 20 minutes before serving.

Decorate with the remaining meringues.

Peach and Mascarpone Gelato

GELATO DI PESCA E MASCARPONE

To ensure the peaches don't lose their fresh colour I churn the gelato as soon as the peaches are puréed and mixed with the mascarpone.

Serves 6–8

160 g/5$\frac{1}{2}$ oz/scant 1 cup caster
   (superfine) sugar
160 ml/5$\frac{1}{2}$ fl oz/generous
   $\frac{2}{3}$ cup water
Juice of $\frac{1}{2}$ lemon
250 g/9 oz/generous 1 cup
   mascarpone
5 ripe peaches

Put the sugar and water in a saucepan and heat gently to dissolve the sugar, about 4 minutes. Swirl the pan around to dislodge any crystals on the bottom, then transfer to a bowl to cool. Add the lemon juice and stir. Put in the refrigerator to chill for 30 minutes.

Pour the chilled sugar syrup into a blender together with the mascarpone and process to combine.

Cut a cross in the stalk end of the peaches and put in a bowl, pour on boiling water and keep pushing them under for 1 minute. Drain and refresh in cold water and the skins will slip off easily. Cut the peaches in half and lift out the stone (pit). Slice directly into the mascarpone mixture in the blender. Process the mixture to a purée.

Churn using an ice cream machine following the manufacturer's instructions until frozen, or still freeze following the method on p.19. Transfer to a freezerproof container, cover and freeze for 6 hours before serving.

If it is frozen for longer and becomes too hard, remove lid and transfer to the refrigerator to soften about 25 minutes before serving.

Left: Gelateria Alla Scala (Doppia Coppia), Trastevere, Rome.

Apricot and Soya Milk Gelato

GELATO DI ALBICOCCA E SOIA

Puréeing the apricots with the well-chilled syrup and soya (soy) milk straight away ensures the flesh does not have time to oxidise and discolour. Choose ripe, sweet apricots not hard, acidic, out-of-season ones. Specialist Itaian shops often sell very good bottled apricots, usually preserved in apricot liqueur, which make a good substitute in this recipe. Simply drain the liquid into a measuring jug (cup) and add enough water to bring it to the same volume of water used in the recipe, then use to make the syrup.

Serves 6–8

130 g/4$\frac{1}{2}$ oz/$\frac{2}{3}$ cup caster
  (superfine) sugar
130 ml/4$\frac{1}{2}$ fl oz/generous
  $\frac{1}{2}$ cup water
300 ml/10 fl oz/1$\frac{1}{4}$ cups
  unsweetened organic soya
  (soy) milk
500 g/1 lb 2 oz ripe apricots

Put the sugar and water in a saucepan and heat gently to dissolve the sugar, about 4 minutes. Swirl the pan around to dislodge any crystals on the bottom, then transfer to a bowl to cool. Mix in the soya (soy) milk and put in the refrigerator to chill for 30 minutes.

Cut the apricots in half and remove the stones (pits). Put half into a blender with half the soya milk mixture and process briefly to combine. Keep cold while processing the rest of the apricots and soya milk mixture and combine both batches.

Churn using an ice cream machine following the manufacturer's instructions until frozen, or still freeze following the method on p.19. Transfer to a freezerproof container, cover and freeze for 6 hours before serving.

If it is frozen for longer and becomes too hard, remove lid and transfer to the refrigerator to soften about 45 minutes before serving.

Liquorice Gelato

GELATO DI LIQUIRIZIA

Liquirizia, a liquorice liqueur from Sorrento, is a good storecupboard ingredient to bring home from a holiday. I love this gelato served with the rather straight scented flavour of a lychee (litchi) sorbetto (p.67). There is something very Italian about this combination. The Italians are so good at marrying different flavours together, which is the reason for the multi-flavoured cones that you can buy in the gelaterias. The flavours in this gelato combination are quite sophisticated so serve in smart separate glasses and guests can spoon a little of each together.

Serves 4–6

600 ml/1 pint/2$\frac{1}{2}$ cups full-
   cream (whole) milk
125 g/4$\frac{1}{2}$ oz soft eating
   liquorice stick, snipped into
   small pieces
6 egg yolks
3 tbsp brown sugar
Pinch of salt
2 tbsp *liquore di liquirizia*
   (liquorice liqueur) (optional)
300 ml/10 fl oz/1$\frac{1}{4}$ cups
   double (heavy) cream

Put the milk and liquorice pieces in a saucepan set over a heat diffuser mat and heat gently to allow the liquorice to melt, about 20 minutes. Keep squashing the liquorice against the side of the pan with a wooden spoon to break it up. It doesn't matter if the liquorice doesn't dissolve totally as it will continue to melt while the custard is being cooked.

Meanwhile, whisk the egg yolks, brown sugar and salt lightly together in a bowl until broken down. Pour the hot liquorice milk over the yolk mixture and whisk together.

Wash out the pan and pour the mixture back in. Cook over a medium heat with a heat diffuser mat under the pan, stirring constantly, for 8–10 minutes. When some of the foam disappears from the surface place a sugar thermometer in the pan and continue to stir until the temperature reads 75°C/167°F. Do not let the mixture get any hotter, otherwise the custard will curdle. Fold in the liqueur. Leave to cool completely, then chill in the refrigerator for 30 minutes.

Whip the cream in a bowl until just floppy then fold into the cold custard. Churn using an ice cream machine following the manufacturer's instructions until frozen, or still freeze following the method on p.19. Transfer to a freezerproof container, cover and freeze for 3 hours before serving.

If it is frozen for longer and becomes too hard, remove lid and transfer to the refrigerator to soften about 20–30 minutes before serving.

Wild Berry Gelato

FRUTTI DI BOSCO

When soft fruit is at its best use whatever is available. The Italian version of this wild berry gelato is often very jam-like, but I prefer a fresher taste and texture. This goes well with other flavours and of course the ubiquitous panna montata *(whipped cream) – just like the super-loaded* cono *in the picture.*

Serves 6

250 g/9 oz mixed berries such as raspberries, redcurrants, blackberries, wild strawberries and blueberries
1 tbsp icing (confectioners') sugar
2–3 tbsp raspberry liqueur
½ quantity of *Gelato di Crema* (Custard Gelato), unchurned and chilled (p.78)

Put the berries and the icing (confectioners') sugar in a pan. Cook over a low heat until the juices start to run, then transfer to a bowl. Crush them a little with a fork to release more juice and leave to cool. Mix in the raspberry liqueur and chill in the refrigerator for 30 minutes.

Mix the chilled fruit into the unchurned *Gelato di Crema*. Churn using an ice cream machine following the manufacturer's instructions until frozen, or still freeze following the method on p.19. Transfer to a freezerproof container, cover and freeze for 4 hours before serving.

If it is frozen for longer and becomes too hard, remove lid and transfer to the refrigerator to soften about 50 minutes before serving.

Overleaf: The Piazza della Cisterna, San Gimignano.

Pine Kernel Gelato

GELATO DI PINOLI

Pine kernels (nuts) in Italy come from ancient trees brought to Sicily by the Moors. The labour intensive process to extract the kernel makes them expensive, but it's worthwhile when you taste this delicious and ever popular gelato. The recipe was given to me by Ben Hirst at Necci dal 1924 Pigneto, Rome. It teams lightly toasted pine kernels with the delicate flavour of acacia honey to make the creamiest iced sensation imaginable. Top with a piece of Croccante *(p.000).*

Serves 6–8

400 ml/14 fl oz/1³/₄ cups full-cream (whole) milk

150 ml/5 fl oz/²/₃ cup whipping cream

150 g/5 oz/scant ¹/₂ cup acacia honey

3 finely pared strips of orange peel

3 coffee beans

4 egg yolks

200 g/7 oz/1¹/₃ cups pine kernels (nuts), lightly toasted (do not over-brown or the flavour will be bitter)

Put the milk, cream and honey in a saucepan together with the orange peel and coffee beans. Heat gently until bubbles appear around the edges of the pan, then remove the pan from the heat.

Whisk the egg yolks in a bowl, pour in the hot milk mixture and stir well. Wash out the pan and pour the mixture back in. Cook over a medium heat with a heat diffuser mat under the pan, stirring constantly, for 8–10 minutes. When some of the foam disappears from the surface place a sugar thermometer in the pan and continue to stir until the temperature reads 75°C/167°F. Do not let the mixture get any hotter, otherwise the custard will curdle. Cool for 1 hour, then strain out the orange rind and coffee beans.

Put 120 g/4¹/₂ oz/scant 1 cup of the pine kernels (nuts) into a blender with a little of the custard and process to a purée, then pour in the rest of the custard. Process briefly until combined. Leave the mixture to cool, then chill in the refrigerator for 30 minutes.

Churn using an ice cream machine following the manufacturer's instructions until frozen, or still freeze following the method on p.19. Transfer to a freezerproof container, cover and freeze for 3 hours before serving.

If it is frozen for longer and becomes too hard, remove lid and transfer to the refrigerator to soften about 30 minutes before serving.

Hazelnut Gelato

GELATO DI NOCCIOLA

This always looks so appealing, in among the display of stainless steel tubs laden with a huge number of different flavours. This is one of my gelateria favourites – its pale creaminess scattered with toasted hazelnuts then drizzled with luscious dark chocolate – it looks and tastes sublime.

Serves 6–8

2 eggs

2 egg yolks

50 g/2 oz/$^1/_4$ cup caster (superfine) sugar

75 g/3 oz/generous $^1/_3$ cup light soft brown sugar

500 ml/16 fl oz/2 cups full-cream (whole) milk

3 tbsp Italian hazelnut liqueur, such as Frangelico

150 g/5 oz/1 cup skinned hazelnuts, toasted and cooled

200 ml/7 fl oz/scant 1 cup double (heavy) cream

50 g/2 oz plain dark (bitter-sweet) chocolate, melted and cooled, but still liquid

Put the eggs, egg yolks, caster (superfine) sugar and 40 g/1$^1/_2$ oz/ scant $^1/_4$ cup of the light soft brown sugar into a large heatproof bowl and whisk together for 1 minute until bubbly.

Pour the milk into a saucepan and heat gently until bubbles appear around the edges of the pan. Pour onto the egg mixture and mix well. Wash out the pan and pour the mixture back in. Cook over a medium heat with a heat diffuser mat under the pan, stirring constantly, for 8–10 minutes. When some of the foam disappears from the surface place a sugar thermometer in the pan and continue to stir until the temperature reads 75°C/167°F. Do not let the mixture get any hotter, otherwise the custard will curdle. Pour into a bowl, add the hazelnut liqueur and leave to cool.

Grind 120 g/4$^1/_2$ oz/generous $^3/_4$ cup of the hazelnuts finely with the remaining light soft brown sugar in a food processor. Set aside the remaining hazelnuts for decoration. Add about one third of the custard to the food processor and process for 1 minute to combine. Add the remaining custard and process again briefly. Transfer to a bowl and chill in the refrigerator for 1 hour.

Pour the mixture through a sieve (strainer) set over a bowl and, using a circular motion, push the solids through with the back of a ladle. Discard what remains in the sieve. Softly whip the cream so it is still loose and fold through the mixture. Churn using an ice cream machine following the manufacturer's instructions until frozen, or still freeze following the method on p.19. Transfer to a freezerproof container, cover and freeze for 6 hours.

Scatter with the reserved hazelnuts and drizzle with melted
chocolate. Transfer to the refrigerator for 10 minutes and serve.
If it is frozen for much longer and becomes too hard, remove lid and
transfer to the refrigerator to soften about 20 minutes before serving.

Right: *Gelato di Nocciola*
in Gelateria di Piazza,
San Gimignano.

Blueberry Gelato

GELATO DI MIRTILLI

This is perfect gelato for a frappe *(p.24) as the yogurt makes it a healthy alternative to full-cream (whole) milk and cream. Use other berries, too for this, such as blackberries, raspberries and strawberries, or blackcurrants when in season.*

Serves 4–6

300 g/10 oz/generous 2 cups
    blueberries
150 g/5 oz/³⁄₄ cup caster
    (superfine) sugar
250 ml/8 fl oz/1 cup water
300 g/10 oz/1 ¹⁄₄ cups organic
    natural (plain) live (bio)
    yogurt (NOT low fat)

Put the blueberries, caster (superfine) sugar and the water into a saucepan and heat gently until the sugar has dissolved and the berries are beginning to give out their juice. Remove the pan from the heat and leave to cool for 30 minutes.

Put the cooled berries and yogurt into a blender and process until the mixture is smooth. Pour into a sieve (strainer) set over a bowl and push the berries through in a circular motion with the back of a ladle. Chill the mixture in the refrigerator for 1 hour.

Churn using an ice cream machine following the manufacturer's instructions until frozen, or still freeze following the method on p.19. Transfer to a freezerproof container, cover and freeze for 3 hours before serving.

If it is frozen for longer and becomes too hard, remove lid and transfer to the refrigerator to soften about 20–30 minutes before serving.

Pistachio Gelato

GELATO DI PISTACCHIO

My friends and I are divided on texture preferences for this gelato. I like the creamy flavour without the grainy bits while others prefer it with the textured quality of the crushed nuts. You can compromise if using the smoother version either by scattering crushed nuts over each serving, or by dipping hand-held cones in a light caramel or chocolate and then into the crushed nuts.

Pistachio nuts arrived in Sicily with the Arabs and the island is the source of the best in Italy. In order to get the fullest flavour, roast the nuts briefly and crush with sugar.

Serves 6–8

160 g/5¼ oz/generous 1 cup
   pistachio nuts, toasted, skins
   rubbed off and cooled
150 g/5 oz/¾ cup caster
   (superfine) sugar
350 ml/12 fl oz/1½ cups full-
   cream (whole) milk
300 ml/10 fl oz/1¼ cups
   double (heavy) cream
½ tsp vanilla extract

Put the nuts and caster (superfine) sugar into a food processor and process until very finely ground. Leave in the machine.

Put the milk and cream in a saucepan and heat gently until bubbles start to appear around the sides of the pan. Pour a little of this mixture onto the pistachios and process again. Add a little more liquid and continue in the same way until all the milky mixture has been used up. Process until very fine. Add the vanilla extract and tip into a large bowl to cool and macerate for a few hours. If you want a coarse texture just pour the liquid over the finely ground mixture in the food processor and process briefly.

Churn using an ice cream machine following the manufacturer's instructions until frozen, or still freeze following the method on p.19. Transfer to a freezerproof container, cover and freeze for 3 hours before serving.

If it is frozen for longer and becomes too hard, remove lid and transfer to the refrigerator to soften about 40 minutes before serving.

If using for frozen layered desserts, process the nuts very finely. Try to buy the best Italian pistachios available, although Iranian ones are also good. These are often sold skinned and sliced in Middle Eastern stores, and are much greener in colour.

Honey Custard Gelato with Marsala

BUONTALENTI

This gelato pays homage to the multi-talented 16th century Florentine architect, Bernardo Buontalenti. He created frozen masterpieces for the Medici court and is said to have been involved in the progressive move from sorbetto to custard-based gelati. To this day a Buontalenti *is on the menu in many gelaterias, its rich eggy creaminess beguilingly flavoured with Marsala wine.*

Serves 8–10

3 tbsp skimmed milk powder

750 ml/1 $\frac{1}{4}$ pints/3 cups full-
   cream (whole) milk

250 ml/9 fl oz/generous 1 cup
   whipping cream

8 large egg yolks

75 g/3 oz/generous $\frac{1}{3}$ cup
   acacia honey

75 g/3 oz/generous $\frac{1}{3}$ cup
   caster (superfine) sugar

4 tbsp Marsala

Whisk the skimmed milk powder into the milk in a saucepan and gently bring to the boil until bubbles start to appear around the side of the pan.

Meanwhile, whisk the egg yolks, honey and sugar together in a heatproof bowl until pale in colour. Pour the hot milk over the egg mixture and stir well.

Wash out the pan and pour the mixture back in. Cook over a medium heat with a heat diffuser mat under the pan, stirring constantly, for 8–10 minutes. When some of the foam disappears from the surface place a sugar thermometer in the pan and continue to stir until the temperature reads 75°C/167°F. Do not let the mixture get any hotter, otherwise the custard will curdle. Transfer to a bowl and leave to cool. Chill in the refrigerator for 1 hour. Mix in the Marsala.

Churn using an ice cream machine following the manufacturer's instructions until frozen, or still freeze following the method on p.19. Transfer to a freezerproof container, cover and freeze for 2 hours before serving.

If it is frozen for longer and becomes too hard, remove lid and transfer to the refrigerator to soften about 25 minutes before serving.

FIOR DI LATTE CON VANIGLIA

This gelato is perfect served with a simple macedonia *– a fresh fruit salad. It is a pure
-tasting gelato, and is quite icy compared to a high fat egg-enriched gelato. The vanilla
can be left out and other flavourings added if wished.*

Serves 6–8

750 ml/1 $^{1}/_{4}$ pints/3 cups full-
cream (whole) milk

100 g/4 oz/generous 1 cup
skimmed milk powder

125 g/4 $^{1}/_{2}$ oz/scant $^{2}/_{3}$ cup
caster (superfine) sugar

25 g/1 oz glucose (dextrose)
powder

1 vanilla pod (bean), split into
two lengthways

Macedonia (fresh fruit salad):
strawberries, raspberries,
redcurrants and blackberries
for example, to serve

Put the milk, milk powder, sugar, glucose (dextrose) and vanilla pod
(bean) in a saucepan and hand whisk together. Bring slowly to
boiling point to dissolve the sugar. When bubbles begin to appear
around the edge of the pan, pour into a large bowl. Squeeze the
seeds from the softened vanilla pod into the liquid, discard the pod
and leave to cool. Chill in the refrigerator for 1 hour.

Churn using an ice cream machine following the manufacturer's
instructions until frozen, or still freeze following the method on p.19.
Transfer to a freezerproof container, cover and freeze for 4 hours
before serving.

If it is frozen for longer and becomes too hard, remove lid and transfer
to the refrigerator to soften about 20 minutes before serving.

Serve with *macedonia* (fresh fruit salad).

Chocolate Chip Gelato

STRACCIATELLA

Everyone loves Stracciatella. *I am told on good authority it is very popular with tourists. Having two comfort foods rolled into one is the most likely reason for this. Experiment – try using* Gelato di Crema *(p.78) as the base gelato or leave the vanilla in the* Fior di Latte *mixture (p.106) if you prefer, but I love the combination below.*

Serves 4

100 g/4 oz good quality plain
    dark (bittersweet) chocolate,
    around 70% cocoa solids
$^1/_2$ quantity *Fior di Latte*
    (p.106), without the vanilla,
    churned

Using a sharp knife, chop the chocolate thinly into 5 mm/$^1/_4$ inch strips, then slice crossways into small chips.

Fold 75 g/3 oz of the chocolate chips into the churned gelato and put in a freezerproof container. Scatter the remainder of the chocolate chips on the top. Freeze for 5 hours.

If frozen for longer and it becomes too hard, remove lid and transfer to the refrigerator 10 minutes before serving to soften.

Above: Gelateria di "Piazza", San Gimignano.

Nougat Gelato

GELATO DI TORRONE

Torrone – *the honey, nuts and egg white sweetmeat that, in essence, has been made since ancient Roman times, was named in the mid-15th century when it was made for a special wedding. As part of the bride's dowry her wealthy father offered the city of Cremona, and as a symbol for the celebration the pastry chefs came up with a replica of the* Torione, *the city's tower.*

Serves 6–8

500 ml/16 fl oz/2 cups full-
   cream (whole) milk

4 egg yolks

100 g/4 oz/generous $^{1}/_{4}$ cup
   runny honey

2 tsp vanilla extract

250 g/9 oz/generous 1 cup
   mascarpone

150 g/5 oz *Torrone di mandorle*
   (almond) or *Torrone di*
   pistacchi (pistachio), see
   Suppliers p.159, snipped
   into tiny pieces with scissors

Icing (confectioners') sugar, for
   dusting the scissors (stops
   the *torrone* sticking)

Pour the milk into a saucepan and heat gently until bubbles appear around the edge of the pan.

Meanwhile, whisk the egg yolks, honey and vanilla extract in a large heatproof bowl until it pale in colour. Pour in the hot milk and stir well.

Wash out the pan and pour the mixture back in. Cook over a medium heat with a heat diffuser mat under the pan, stirring constantly, for 8–10 minutes. When some of the foam disappears from the surface place a sugar thermometer in the pan and continue to stir until the temperature reads 75°C/167°F. Do not let the mixture get any hotter, otherwise the custard will curdle. Pour the custard into a bowl and leave to cool. Chill in the refrigerator for 30 minutes.

Put the mascarpone into another bowl and add the custard, a little at a time, whisking in between each addition until smooth.

Churn using an ice cream machine following the manufacturer's instructions until frozen, then fold in the *torrone*, or still freeze following the method on p.19, then fold in the *torrone*. Transfer to a freezerproof container, cover and freeze for 2 hours before serving.

If it is frozen for longer and becomes too hard, remove lid and transfer to the refrigerator to soften about 30 minutes before serving.

Mango Gelato

GELATO DI MANGO

A silky smooth, sensual kind of gelato. I prefer to eat it straight from the ice cream machine when it's still slightly soft and voluptuous. For a party, start freezing the mixture in the machine as the appetizer is served, then take it out and pop into the freezer until you are ready for dessert. Just serve it straight from the bucket into little bowls with chiacchere – the crisply fried pasta shapes known as "gossips", although in Rome they are called "frappe" (p.148).

Serves 4–6

5 ripe mangoes, about
    300 g/10 oz each (golden
    mangoes give a good colour)
Juice of 2 limes
150 g/5 oz/$^{3}/_{4}$ cup caster
    (superfine) sugar
150 ml/5 fl oz/$^{2}/_{3}$ cup water
300 ml/10 fl oz/1$^{1}/_{4}$ cups
    double (heavy) cream
Pinch of salt

Using a sharp knife, slice the mango cheeks from each side of the stone (seed). Put in a food processor and process until smooth. Pass the mixture through a sieve (strainer) into a bowl and press through in a circular motion with the back of a ladle. Discard the fibres left in the sieve.

Put the caster (superfine) sugar and water in a saucepan and heat gently to allow the sugar to dissolve, about 4 minutes. Swirl the liquid around the pan to dislodge any sugar crystals on the bottom. Transfer to a bowl and cool. Strain the syrup over the mango purée and mix in together with the double (heavy) cream and salt. Mix well until combined. Chill in the refrigerator for 30 minutes.

Churn using an ice cream machine following the manufacturer's instructions until frozen, or still freeze following the method on p.19. Transfer to a freezerproof container, cover and freeze for 2 hours before serving.

If it is frozen for longer and becomes too hard, remove lid and transfer to the refrigerator to soften about 45 minutes before serving.

GELATO DI CIOCCOLATO BIANCO CON VANIGLIA

Sergio Dondole from the famed artisan Gelateria d'Piazza in the medieval hilltop town of San Gimignano showed me his trick of pulverizing top quality whole vanilla pods (beans) with sugar. He uses the result in his wonderful gelato creations. So, inspired by his idea, I made this rich indulgent gelato using the very best quality ingredients, something he always insists upon.

Serves 6

1 whole vanilla pod (bean), cut
   into lengths
125 g/4$^{1}/_{2}$ oz/scant $^{2}/_{3}$ cup
   caster (superfine) sugar
4 egg yolks
500 ml/16 fl oz/2 cups full-
   cream (whole) milk
250 ml/9 fl oz/generous 1 cup
   double (heavy) cream
100 g/4 oz good quality white
   chocolate

Using a "wet and dry" grinder (see Suppliers on p.159), pulverize the vanilla pod (bean) and sugar together in 2 batches. Alternatively, process in a coffee grinder.

Whisk the egg yolks and half the vanilla sugar together in a large heatproof bowl. Put the remaining vanilla sugar in a saucepan with the milk and cream and gently heat to dissolve the sugar. As soon as bubbles begin to appear around the sides of the pan, pour into the egg yolk mixture and mix well.

Wash out the pan and pour the mixture back in. Cook over a medium heat with a heat diffuser mat under the pan, stirring constantly, for 8–10 minutes. When some of the foam disappears from the surface place a sugar thermometer in the pan and continue to stir until the temperature reads 75°C/167°F. Do not let the mixture get any hotter, otherwise the custard will curdle. Remove the pan from the heat, break the white chocolate into the mixture and stir well to melt. Pour into a bowl and leave to cool, then chill in the refrigerator for 30 minutes.

Churn using an ice cream machine following the manufacturer's instructions until frozen, or still freeze following the method on p.19. Transfer to a freezerproof container, cover and freeze for 8 hours before serving.

If it is frozen for longer and becomes too hard, remove lid and transfer to the refrigerator to soften about 20–30 minutes before serving.

Rum and Raisin Gelato

MALAGA

Despite the connotations as to the roots of this gelato it is very popular in the gelaterias. Quite unbelievably "Moorish" in every way, its rich velvety texture with lots of sweetness and alcohol means it never gets too hard no matter how long it is kept in the freezer (although the ice crystals will build up and the flavour will inevitably suffer if left for too long). I still prefer to temper the icy-ness in the refrigerator for a brief while before serving it.

Serves 4–6

100 g/4 oz/scant ²/₃ cup raisins

90 ml/3 fl oz/¹/₃ cup dark rum

500 ml/16 fl oz/2 cups full-cream (whole) milk

4 egg yolks

100 g/4 oz/¹/₂ cup light soft brown sugar

2 tsp vanilla extract

250 g/9 oz/generous 1 cup mascarpone

Soak the raisins in the rum for 1 hour or overnight.

Pour the milk into a saucepan and heat gently until bubbles appear around the edge of the pan.

Whisk the egg yolks, sugar and vanilla extract together in a large heatproof bowl until pale in colour. Pour in the hot milk and stir well. Wash out the pan and pour the mixture back in. Cook over a medium heat with a heat diffuser mat under the pan, stirring constantly, for 8–10 minutes. When some of the foam disappears from the surface place a sugar thermometer in the pan and continue to stir until the temperature reads 75°C/167°F. Do not let the mixture get any hotter, otherwise the custard will curdle. Pour the custard into a bowl and leave to cool. Chill in the refrigerator for 30 minutes.

Put the mascarpone into a bowl and add the custard, a little at a time, whisking in between each addition until smooth. Strain the rum from the raisins over the custard and mix well. Set the raisins aside.

Churn using an ice cream machine following the manufacturer's instructions until frozen, or still freeze following the method on p.19. Transfer to a freezerproof container, cover and freeze overnight. Serve the next day. Transfer to the refrigerator about 15 minutes before serving.

Orange/Lemon Gelato

GELATO DI ARANCIA/LIMONE

In the Gelateria Giolitti in the Via degli Uffici del Vicario, close to the Pantheon in Rome, these gelati are always served with long wafers called Cialdone *with various other ices and a glass of water on the side. Now run by Nazzareno Giolitti, this very beautiful and smart establishment has been around since 1900. Sit outside, having chosen from the huge mouthwatering assortment, to eat your ice and watch the world stroll by.*

Serves 4

For Gelato di Arancia

¹/₂ quantity of *Gelato di Crema* (Custard Gelato), unchurned and chilled (p.78)

Juice of 2 large oranges (300 ml/10 fl oz/1¹/₄ cups), retaining the juicy bits

2 tbsp Cointreau

Pinch of salt

For Gelato di Limone

¹/₂ quantity of *Gelato di Crema* (Custard Gelato), unchurned and chilled (p.78)

Juice of 2 large lemons (125 ml/4 fl oz/¹/₂ cup)

Pinch of salt

To make the Gelato di Arancia, put the *Gelato di Crema* into a large bowl and stir in the orange juice, Cointreau and salt.

To make the Gelato di Limone, put the *Gelato di Crema* into a large bowl and stir in the lemon juice and salt.

Churn using an ice cream machine following the manufacturer's instructions until frozen, or still freeze following the method on p.19. Transfer to a freezerproof container, cover and freeze for 4 hours before serving.

If it is frozen for longer and becomes too hard, remove lid and transfer to the refrigerator to soften about 20–30 minutes before serving.

GELATO DI ZUCCA E AMARETTI

Inspired by the famous ravioli stuffing mixture, these flavours go amazingly well together. A memorable gelato. You could use butternut squash in place of the pumpkin.

Serves 6-8

550 g/1 lb 4 oz pumpkin,
  about 375 g/12$^{1}/_{2}$ oz in
  weight when peeled and
  deseeded (alternatively use
  butternut squash)
85 g/3$^{1}/_{2}$ oz/generous $^{1}/_{4}$ cup
  caster (superfine) sugar
3 egg yolks
250 ml/9 fl oz/generous 1 cup
  full-cream (whole) milk
150 ml/5 fl oz/$^{2}/_{3}$ cup
  whipping cream
75 g/3 oz traditional hard
  amaretti cookies,
  processed finely

Cut the pumpkin into chunks and steam for about 20 minutes until soft. Transfer to a blender and process until a purée forms. Tip it into a nylon sieve (strainer) set over a bowl and push it through in a circular motion with the back of a ladle. Set aside until required.

Whisk the sugar and egg yolks together in a large heatproof bowl until pale in colour. Put the milk and cream in a saucepan and bring to the boil. As soon as bubbles appear around the edge of the pan, pour into the egg mixture and mix well.

Wash out the pan and pour the mixture back in. Cook over a medium heat with a heat diffuser mat under the pan, stirring constantly, for 8–10 minutes. When some of the foam disappears from the surface place a sugar thermometer in the pan and continue to stir until the temperature reads 75°C/167°F. Do not let the mixture get any hotter, otherwise the custard will curdle. Remove from the heat and pour into a bowl. Mix in the amaretti and leave to cool.

Mix in the pumpkin purée and chill in the refrigerator for 30 minutes.

Churn using an ice cream machine following the manufacturer's instructions until frozen, or still freeze following the method on p.19. Transfer to a freezerproof container, cover and freeze for 4 hours before serving.

If it is frozen for longer and becomes too hard, remove lid and transfer to the refrigerator to soften about 45 minutes before serving.

Kiwi Gelato

GELATO DI KIWI

Kiwis originated in China but now grow in Italy, as well as other countries worldwide. The fruit provides twice as much vitamin C as an orange. Do look for ripe and ready kiwis for this gelato.

Serves 6–8

200 g/7 oz/1 cup caster
   (superfine) sugar
50 g/2 oz glucose (dextrose)
   powder
250 ml/9 fl oz/generous 1 cup
   water
Juice of 4 limes
8 large kiwi fruit,
   about 900 g/2 lb in total
200 ml/7 fl oz/scant 1 cup
   whipping cream

Put the sugar and water in a saucepan and heat gently to dissolve the sugar, about 4 minutes. Swirl the pan around to dislodge any crystals on the bottom, then transfer to a bowl to cool. Add the lime juice and stir to combine.

Meanwhile, cut the kiwi fruits in half horizontally and scoop the flesh out into a blender. Process until a purée forms. You can leave in the black seeds but I prefer to take them out. Pour into a nylon sieve (strainer) set over a bowl and push the fruit through in a circular motion using the back of a ladle.

Combine the purée, sugar syrup and the cream in a large bowl and chill in the refrigerator for 30 minutes.

Churn using an ice cream machine following the manufacturer's instructions until frozen, or still freeze following the method on p.19. Transfer to a freezerproof container, cover and freeze for 4 hours before serving.

If it is frozen for longer and becomes too hard, remove lid and transfer to the refrigerator to soften about 30 minutes before serving.

  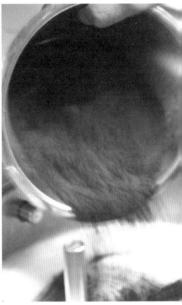

  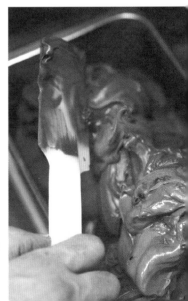

Chocolate Gelato

GELATO DI CIOCCOLATO

Sergio Dondole, owner of the renowned Gelateria d'Piazza in the medieval hilltop town of San Gimignano, showed me this truly wonderful recipe. He insists that it is much better left until the next day to allow the flavours to develop. Having tasted it I agree, but as this is homemade you can leave the mixture to mature ahead of freezing. Experiment using the instructions below to ensure a soft gelato ready in time for dessert.

Serves 8–10

2 whole eggs

4 egg yolks

150 g/5 oz/³/₄ cup caster
(superfine) sugar

1 litre/1³/₄ pints/4 cups full-
cream (whole) milk

25 g/1 oz glucose (dextrose)
powder

85 g unsweetened organic
cocoa powder, sifted twice

50 g plain dark (bittersweet)
chocolate, finely sliced into
chards

Pinch of salt

2 tbsp Grappa

Put the eggs, yolks and half the caster (superfine) sugar into a bowl and whisk together for 1 minute until thoroughly mixed.

Put the milk, the rest of the sugar and glucose (dextrose) powder in a saucepan and heat gently until the sugar dissolves. Increase the heat and when bubbles appear around the edges of the pan pour onto the egg mixture and mix well.

Wash out the pan and pour the mixture back in. Cook over a medium heat with a heat diffuser mat under the pan, stirring constantly, for 8–10 minutes. When some of the foam disappears from the surface place a sugar thermometer in the pan and continue to stir until the temperature reads 75°C/167°F. Do not let the mixture get any hotter, otherwise the custard will curdle.

Sift the cocoa powder again over the custard together with the chocolate and salt and whisk well until smooth and the chocolate melted. Pour the mixture into a nylon sieve (strainer) set over a bowl and press with the back of a ladle using a circular motion. Leave to cool. Add the Grappa and chill in the refrigerator for 1 hour.

Churn using an ice cream machine following the manufacturer's instructions until frozen, or still freeze following the method on p.19. Transfer to a freezerproof container, cover and freeze for 3 hours before serving. If it is frozen for longer and becomes too hard, remove lid and transfer to the refrigerator to soften about 45 minutes before serving.

ICED DESSERTS

PACIUGO

In the Genoese dialect paciugo *means something of a messy concoction, in Italian it translates to* pasticcio. *I was told about this sundae-like dessert by Livia Rolandini who knew it well in 1950s Portofino, when girls with tiny waists wore Capri pants and head-scarves tied at the back, Liz Taylor-style, to be driven at high speeds in Alfa Romeos.*

Makes 2

150 ml/5 fl oz/$^{2}/_{3}$ cup double
   (heavy) cream
200 g/7 oz raspberries, crushed
   with a fork
4 scoops *Gelato di Fragole*,
   softened as the recipe (p.80)
2 scoops *Gelato di Crema*,
   softened as the recipe (p.78)
2 tbsp roughly chopped
   pistachio nuts

To serve
Fresh cherries
Chocolate and vanilla-striped
   wafer cigars

Whip the cream in a bowl until soft peaks form, then transfer to a piping (pastry) bag fitted with a 1.5 cm/$^{5}/_{8}$ inch star nozzle (tip).

Place about a quarter of the crushed raspberries in the bottom of each serving glass followed by two scoops per glass of *Gelato di Fragole*. Place a scoop of *Gelato di Crema* on top.

Divide the remaining crushed raspberries between the two glasses then scatter with chopped pistachios.

Pipe some cream decoratively on the top, then add a cherry and some wafer cigars and serve.

Cassata

SEMIFREDDO DI CASSATA

I use this cassata *mixture as a filling for several domed recipes. It is just as delicious served straight from the freezer as part of an assortment of gelati for a dinner party dessert.*

Serves 4–6

200 g/7 oz/scant 1 cup
   candied peel or a mixture
   of candied chopped fruits
284 ml/scant 10 fl oz/scant
   1 ¼ cups whipping cream
50 ml/2 fl oz/¼ cup Strega
   liqueur
100 g/4 oz/½ cup caster
   (superfine) sugar
1 sachet dried egg white
   powder (p.159)

Chop the candied peel finely and set aside.

Put the cream, Strega and half the sugar in a bowl and whip until it holds a shape. Reconstitute and whisk the dried egg white following the packet instructions. Gradually whisk in the remaining sugar until soft peaks form.

Fold the two mixtures together gently then fold in the chopped candied peel or fruits. Transfer to a freezerproof container and freeze overnight. Before serving, remove the lid and transfer to the refrigerator for 5 minutes.

Tip: Sundora is a good brand of candied peel and is widely available (p.159). Strega is a liqueur flavoured with herbs and saffron. It is also widely available.

Truffle

TARTUFO

This is a very popular dessert made by Mauro Petrini at Gelateria Petrini in Rome. The best chocolate gelato must be used for this recipe. An Amarene cherry is permissible pushed into the centre of the ball before rolling in good quality chopped chocolate. Tre Scalini in Piazza Navona near the Pantheon serve Tartufo *with* panna montata *(softly whipped cream) and a chocolate wafer (see p.121).*

Serves 8

¹/₂ quantity of *Gelato di Cioccolato* (p.119), churned, frozen then softened slightly in the refrigerator, if necessary

8 Amarene cherries in syrup, drained

125 g/4¹/₂ oz plain dark (bittersweet) chocolate

142 ml/scant 5 fl oz/scant ²/₃ cup whipping cream

Using a ball scoop, make 8 scoops of chocolate gelato and put onto a tray. Push a cherry into the underside of each scoop and re-freeze for 30 minutes.

Chop the chocolate into small pieces and put into a sieve (strainer) set over a bowl. Shake it to loosen all the dust size pieces of chocolate. Put the larger pieces on a tray and roll the balls of gelato in them until they are evenly coated. Freeze for 15 minutes.

To serve, whip the cream in a large bowl and either pipe the cream using a star nozzle (tip) or spoon it onto the *tartufo*. Transfer to the refrigerator 15 minutes before serving to soften.

BISCUIT TORTONI

This early 19th-century dessert of temptation was invented in honour of the famous Italian founder of the Parisian Café Tortoni (known as the Café Velloni before Guiseppe Tortoni bought and turned it into what became a famous gelato parlour). "Biscuit" was the term used to describe an oblong shape. The texture of the dessert is soft and creamy because of the zabaioni mixture and whipped cream that are folded in.

Serves 8

Sunflower oil, for oiling

110 g/4¼ oz crispy amaretti
   biscuits (cookies)
   or macaroons

2 eggs

3 tbsp Amaretto liqueur

50 g/2 oz/¼ cup caster
   (superfine) sugar

Pinch of salt

375 ml/13 fl oz/generous
   1½ cups whipping cream

4 tbsp skinned and toasted
   almonds, finely chopped

Prepare a small 450 g/1 lb loaf tin (pan) by brushing over with oil and lining with clingfilm (plastic wrap), letting the excess overhang the sides. Alternatively, individually wrap the bases of 8 x 7 cm (3 in) ring moulds with clingfilm. Put the amaretti biscuits (cookies) into a large plastic food bag and roughly crush with the end of a rolling pin.

Put the eggs, Amaretto liqueur, sugar and salt in a large heatproof bowl set over a saucepan of simmering water (the base of the bowl should not come into contact with the water) and whisk until the mixture doubles in volume. (You can use electric beaters, but remember to wrap the cable round your arm so it doesn't make contact with the heat source.) Remove the bowl from the pan and continue to whisk until the mixture leaves a thick trail when the whisks are lifted out. Place in the refrigerator to chill.

Whip the cream in another bowl until it is the same thickness as the egg mixture. Then, using a large metal spoon, fold this into the cooled egg mixture. Gently fold in the amaretti and nuts, taking care not to lose any volume. Spoon the mixture into the prepared loaf tin or moulds and fold over the excess clingfilm to cover the top. Transfer to the freezer for 24 hours.

When ready to serve, wrap a warm, damp cloth around the sides of the tin or moulds and turn out onto serving plates. Transfer to the refrigerator 5–8 minutes before serving.

port at Ostia. Plans of great public buildings to be erected
at Alexandria or in Rome were being submitted to him ;
or, again, he was arranging for the establishment of pu...
libraries in various parts of the capital. Meanw...
preparations for the Parthian war must have ...
greater part of his time ; for the campaig...
vast character. So sure was he that it ...
years or more that he framed a law ...
magistrates and public officials fo...
should be appointed before hi...
insured the tranquility of R...
absence in the East, thus leav...
arms into remote lands wh...
capital might be almost i...
that Cæsar's recent camp...
months' or weeks' duration...
vici now represented his n...
these plans for a three ...
me to indicate clearly th...
himself to the conquest ...
Alexander's footsteps ...
Rome laden with the lo...
have pictured himself e...
war as the conqueror of ...
no doubt in his mind u...
then accept with enthu...
the world.

As the weeks went by, ...
monarchy became more cl...
seem to have considered it ...
assumption of the sovereign...
war, since his long absence ...
elevation to the throne might ...
office. Moreover, a strong feelin...
his contemplated assumption of ro...
have been aware that he could not put...
tion without considerable opposition.
that " his desire of being king had brough...
most apparent and mortal hatred—a fact w...
the most plausible pretence to those who had bee...
secret enemies all along." Much adverse comment had
been made with reference to his not rising to receive the
Senatorial deputation ; and indeed, he felt it necessary to

make excuses for his action, saying that his old illness was
upon him at the time. A report was spread that he himself
w...ld have been willing to rise, but that Balbus had said
..." Will you not remember you are Cæsar and claim
...e to your merit ? " and it was further related
...Dictator had realised the offence he had
...his throat to his friends, and had told
...ly to lay down his life if the public
...ncidents such as this showed that
...ly favourable for his *coup* ; and
...to consider its postponement.
...mething to be said in favour
...must have been more or less
...if it were urged upon him
...The position of Cleopatra,
...some anxiety. Without
...n of an hereditary mon-
...own wife, Calpurnia,
...with an heir, and there
...ome who could be ex-
... any degree of success,
...production of sons and
...as he to rid himself of
...ithout offending public
...ngship at once and make
...f sustaining with success
...de for three years while
...uld it not be much wiser
...his period, there to await
...r and to ascend the throne
...During his absence in the
...mently meet with a sudden and
...uld dare to attribute her death
...y's ingenuity.
...w made, or confirmed, in view of
...learly that his desire for the monarchy
...with his present marital conditions.
...n and a son and heir there could be little
...ating a throne, since already he had been made
...te autocrat for his lifetime ; for unless the office was
to be handed on without dispute to his son Cæsarion, there
was no advantage in striving for an immediate elevation
to the kingship. By his will, therefore, which was made

MOKA SEMIFREDDO

This luscious parfait is made from crushed dark chocolate-covered espresso beans and a frothy light egg and cream whisked mousse mixture. It needs no churning.

Put the sugar and espresso in a saucepan and heat gently to dissolve the sugar. Increase the heat and boil for 3 minutes.

Put the chocolate-covered coffee beans in a small grinding machine (or you could use a food processor) and process until finely ground. Tip into a bowl and leave to chill in the refrigerator until needed. Meanwhile, whisk the egg yolks lightly in a bowl to break them up.

Gradually pour the hot sugar syrup onto the egg yolks whisking with electric beaters. Increase the speed and whisk constantly for 5 minutes until the mixture is cool, has increased in volume and leaves a thick trail when the beaters are lifted out of the mixture. Place in the refrigerator to chill.

Whip the cream in another bowl until slightly thickened (leaving a trail when the beaters are lifted). If the cream is any stiffer it is difficult to fold into the egg mixture without losing volume. Using a large metal spoon, gently fold the cream through the egg mixture and then fold in the crushed chocolate-covered coffee beans. Spoon the mixture into a freezerproof container, cover, and freeze for about 4 hours.

If freezing for longer, remove lid and transfer to the refrigerator 15 minutes before serving to soften slightly. To serve, spoon into glasses, cups or pots and freeze again for 15 minutes. Decorate the tops with the chocolate shards.

Serves 6

100 g/4 oz/$^1/_2$ cup caster (superfine) sugar

185 ml/6$^1/_2$ fl oz/generous $^3/_4$ cup strong freshly brewed espresso

6 egg yolks

3 heaped tbsp dark (bittersweet) chocolate-covered coffee beans

300 ml/10 fl oz/1$^1/_4$ cups double (heavy) cream

25 g/1 oz good quality plain dark (bittersweet) chocolate, cut into shards to decorate

Sicilian Gelato Cake

CASSATA SICILIANA

This festive Sicilian dome-shaped dessert was decreed enough of a classic to get its own standard recipe for a gelato version. The dome shape is created by lining a bowl with vanilla gelato, followed by a layer of pistachio and a layer of alcohol-soaked Pan di Spagna, *Italy's fatless sponge cake. The centre is then filled with a cassata mixture and chopped chocolate and candied or glacé fruits, topped with another layer of pistachio and vanilla. If you wish, you can decorate this frozen delight with rosettes of whipped cream and candied orange peel (as is traditional).*

Serves 6

3/4 quantity of *Gelato di Crema* (p.78) churned, frozen, then allowed to
soften a little in the refrigerator

1/2 quantity of *Gelato di Pistacchio* (p.103) churned, frozen, then allowed to
soften a little in the refrigerator

40 g/1 1/4 oz *Pan di Spagna*, (p.154), cut into triangles, or sponge fingers

3 tbsp rum

25 g/1 oz dark (bittersweet) chocolate, chopped

1/2 quantity of *Semifreddo di Cassata* (p.124) made with rum instead of Strega

When the *Gelato di Crema* is pliable, use it to line a 1.25 litre/ 2 pint/1 quart bowl to a thickness of about 1.5 cm/3/4 inch, then freeze for 45 minutes. Repeat with the *Gelato di Pistacchio* and re-freeze for a further 45 minutes.

Using a pastry brush, brush the sponge triangles or fingers with the rum and arrange in a layer on top of the pistachio gelato. Fold the chopped chocolate into the *Semifreddo di Cassata* and pile the mixture into the centre. Finish with a layer of pistachio then a layer of *Gelato di Crema*. Smooth over the top and cover with clingfilm (plastic wrap) and freeze overnight.

One hour and 40 minutes before serving unmould the cassata by dipping the bowl carefully into hot water to loosen the gelato. Wipe the bowl and invert onto a serving dish. Give it a sharp tap and it will fall out. Wipe any melted gelato from around the base and freeze for 90 minutes.

Take out of the freezer and put in the fridge for about 10 minutes. Transfer to a serving plate, cut into 6 wedges and serve.

Soft-scoop Pick-Me-Up

SEMIFREDDO DI TIRAMISÙ

All the gelaterias have this famous Italian dessert-turned-gelato. I have put it into the dessert section because a basic gelato is combined with a zabaione mixture and mascarpone and then frozen. If timed just right, this should provide the perfect consistency – easily scoopable but still icy, and complete with soft sponge fingers.

Serves 8

For the zabaione mixture

160 g/5$^{1}/_{2}$ oz/generous
   $^{3}/_{4}$ cup caster (superfine)
   sugar

160 ml/5$^{1}/_{2}$ fl oz/$^{2}/_{3}$ cup water

4 egg yolks

6 tbsp Marsala

250 g/9 oz/generous 1 cup
   mascarpone

1 quantity *Gelato di Crema*
   mixture, unchurned (p.78)

80 ml/2$^{3}/_{4}$ fl oz/scant
   $^{1}/_{3}$ cup espresso

25 g/1 oz/$^{1}/_{8}$ cup caster
   (superfine) sugar

1 tbsp Marsala

12 sponge fingers (ladyfingers)

To serve

Cocoa powder, sifted, to dust

50 g/2 oz dark (bittersweet)
   chocolate, at room
   temperature

Panna montata (softly
   whipped cream)

To make the zabaione, put the sugar and water in a saucepan and heat gently for about 4 minutes to dissolve the sugar. Swirl the pan around to dislodge any crystals on the bottom, then increase the heat and bring to the boil until the sugar syrup reaches 121°C/250°F on a sugar thermometer.

Put the egg yolks and Marsala in a heatproof bowl set over a pan of simmering water (do not let the bowl touch the water) and whisk together. (If you use electric beaters, ensure the cable is secured around your arm and kept away from the heat source.) Whisk in the hot syrup in a slow, steady stream then continue to whisk until the mixture has doubled in volume and is thick enough for the beaters to leave a firm trail when lifted out of the mixture. Remove the bowl from the heat and place it in a bowl of cold water. Continue to whisk until the mixture has cooled and is even thicker. Leave to chill in the refrigerator for 30 minutes.

Place the mascarpone in a bowl and blend in the *Gelato di Crema* mixture, a little at a time. Fold in the chilled zabaione. Churn using an ice cream machine following the manufacturer's instructions. You may need to do this in 2 batches, then transfer the mixture to a container and freeze. Alternatively, still freeze following the method on p.19. The mixture is easiest to use after it has been churned and put in the freezer for 3 hours. Or, in the case of still freezing, 2 hours in the freezer after the last blending.

Put the espresso and sugar in a saucepan and heat gently to dissolve the sugar, then leave to cool. Stir in the Marsala and chill until needed.

Spoon one-third of the gelato mixture into a large freezerproof container with a capacity of at least 1.5 litre/$2^{1}/_{2}$ pints/$6^{1}/_{3}$ cups. Take half the sponge fingers and dip one at a time into the espresso syrup, shaking off any excess, and arrange over the gelato. Repeat with a further one-third of the gelato and the remaining fingers. Finish with a top layer of gelato. Freeze for 3 hours. If it is frozen for longer and becomes too hard transfer to the refrigerator for about 30 minutes before serving to soften the sponge.

When ready to serve, dust the top with cocoa, then decorate with curls of chocolate shaved from the block using a vegetable peeler. Serve with *panna montata* (softly whipped cream).

Citrus and Saffron Semifreddo

SPONGADA DI AGRUMI E ZAFFERANO

This tangy semifreddo, called a spongada, *is a soft cream-based Italian dessert – in this case with a citrus flavouring. You can freeze it in little glasses but I like to scoop it into serving dishes straight from the freezer as the combination of ingredients prevents it freezing solid, making it a useful dessert to bring out at a moment's notice.*

Serves 6–8

1 lime

1 lemon

150 g/5 oz/³⁄₄ cup caster
   (superfine) sugar

75 ml/2¹⁄₂ fl oz/scant ¹⁄₃ cup
   water

2 egg whites

150 ml/5 fl oz/²⁄₃ cup double
   (heavy) cream

³⁄₄ tsp saffron threads soaked in
   2 tsp boiling water for
   1 hour

Squeeze the juice from the lime and lemon and put in a large bowl with 50 g/2 oz/¹⁄₄ cup of the sugar and set aside. Put the remaining sugar and the water into a small saucepan and heat gently to dissolve the sugar, about 4 minutes. Swirl the liquid around the pan to dislodge any sugar crystals still on the bottom. Increase the heat and boil to a temperature of 116°C/240°F (the soft ball stage) on a sugar thermometer.

Meanwhile, whisk the egg whites in a clean bowl until they form soft peaks. Gradually whisk in the hot syrup (avoiding the blades), and continue to whisk until the mixture cools down (about 6 minutes). Place in the refrigerator to chill.

Add the cream to the citrus juice and sugar mixture in the bowl and whisk together until soft peaks form. Using a large metal spoon, carefully fold the cooled meringue mixture into the cream mixture, so as not to lose any volume.

Spoon the mixture into a freezerproof container and carefully fold in the saffron to create an uneven yellow colour. Try not to over-mix. Cover and freeze for a minimum of 4 and a maximum of 24 hours. Serve scooped straight from the freezer.

Note: If you want the saffron colour but without the filaments simply strain before using the liquid.

Vanilla and Coffee Dome

SPUMONE DI CAFFÈ E VANIGLIA

A spumone *is made in a* stampo da spumoni *– a specially designed dome-shaped mould with a lid. Many of these desserts date back to the medieval period, when it was fashionable to make replicas of the many domed churches, and the dome is still a popular shape for Italian desserts. The* spumoni *has two layers of gelato and a semifreddo filling that never gets completely rock hard.*

Serves 6

$^1/_2$ quantity *Gelato di Crema* mixture (p.78), churned and frozen, then softened slightly in the refrigerator

$^1/_2$ quantity of *Gelato di Caffè* (p.84), churned and frozen, then softened slightly in the refrigerator

35 g/1$^1/_4$ oz/scant $^1/_4$ cup dried figs, chopped into small pieces

35 g/1$^1/_4$ oz/scant $^1/_4$ cup dried, ready-to-eat apricots

15 g/$^1/_2$ oz/scant $^1/_8$ cup pistachio nuts, roughly chopped

$^1/_2$ quantity of *Semifreddo di Cassata* (p.124), without the candied fruit, frozen

For the espresso sauce

250 g/9 oz/1$^1/_4$ cups caster (superfine) sugar

125 ml/4 fl oz/$^1/_2$ cup strong espresso

2 tbsp Frangelico liqueur

To make the espresso sauce, put the ingredients into a saucepan and heat gently for about 4 minutes to dissolve the sugar. Increase the heat and boil until reduced to a thick syrup. Leave to cool then chill until needed.

When the gelato is pliable line the sides of a 1.25 litre/2 pint/5 cup capacity bowl with the *Gelato di Crema* to about 1.5 cm/$^5/_8$ inch thick leaving a hole in the middle. Freeze for 45 minutes. Repeat with the *Gelato di Caffè* and refreeze for a further 45 minutes. Add the chopped fruits and pistachios to the *Semifreddo di Cassata* and spoon into the remaining hole in the centre. Smooth the top, cover with clingfilm (plastic wrap) and freeze overnight.

One hour and 40 minutes before serving unmould the dessert by dipping the bowl carefully into hot water to loosen the gelato. Wipe the bowl and invert onto a small board or tray. Give it a sharp tap and it will fall out. Wipe any melted gelato from around the base and freeze for 1$^1/_2$ hours.

Remove from the freezer and transfer to the refrigerator for about 10 minutes. Transfer to a serving plate, cut into 6 wedges and serve with the espresso sauce.

Meringue Ice Cream Cake

TORTA DI MERINGA

This is one of the occasions when using bitter chocolate is just right because of the sweetness of the meringue. Usually artisan gelato makers prefer chocolate with a sweeter flavour.

Serves 6–8

250 g/9 oz/generous 1 cup
  mascarpone
25 g/1 oz/$^1/_8$ cup caster
  (superfine) sugar
100 g/4 oz good quality plain
  dark (bittersweet) chocolate
150 ml/5 fl oz/$^2/_3$ cup double
  (heavy) cream
2 tbsp grappa
75 g/3 oz/$^3/_4$ cup walnuts,
  roughly chopped
100 g/4 oz chocolate-dipped
  orange pieces (*aranciotti*),
  chopped

For the meringue
3 egg whites
Pinch of salt
175 g/6 oz/scant 1 cup caster
  (superfine) sugar
Cocoa powder, for dusting

Preheat the oven 140°C/275°F/Gas Mark 1.

For the meringue, draw 3 circles, about 18 cm/7 inches diameter, onto a piece of non-stick baking paper (baking parchment). Turn the paper over and place on baking (cookie) sheets.

Whisk the egg whites and salt together in a large grease-free bowl until firm peaks form. Whisk in the sugar, a few tablespoons at a time, whisking well between each addition, until the meringue is glossy and stands in firm peaks. Spread a third of the mixture evenly into the circles, just up to the drawn edges. Bake for 30 minutes then carefully turn them over and cook for a further 10 minutes.

Meanwhile, whisk the mascarpone and sugar together in a large bowl. Place the chocolate in a heatproof bowl set over a saucepan of hot water and leave until melted. Remove the bowl from the pan and leave to cool for 15 minutes, then fold into the mascarpone mixture.

Whip the double (heavy) cream and grappa together in a bowl until the cream holds a firm trail when the beaters are removed. Fold into the mascarpone mixture. Remove a third of this mix and set aside in the refrigerator. Stir the nuts and orange pieces into the remainder.

Put a layer of the meringue into a 18 cm/7 inch springform cake tin, then add a layer of the nutty mascarpone mixture. Repeat the layers ending with a top layer of meringue. If the meringue breaks just patch it, but try to keep the top one intact. Freeze overnight.

Unmould onto a plate and, using the reserved mascarpone mixture, fill in any gaps in the sides and smooth over. Freeze for 30 minutes. Transfer to the refrigerator 15 minutes before serving. Dust with cocoa.

PEZZI DURI

Pezzi Duri literally means "hard pieces" and dates back to the 18th century. The blocks of frozen gelato were sliced and individually wrapped in greaseproof (waxed) paper like sweeties (candies). This idea predates the Neapolitan block. Any number of lines of gelato or sorbetto could be piped between layers of firm Gelato di Crema *(Custard Gelato). I like to serve this with scoops of the sorbetto flavours I have used in the* Pezzi Duri.

Serves 6–8

$^{1}/_{2}$ quantity of *Gelato di Crema* (p.78)

$^{1}/_{2}$ quantity of *Sorbetto di Mango* (p.53)

$^{1}/_{2}$ quantity of *Sorbetto di Lamponi* (p.48)

Line a 1 kg/2$^{1}/_{4}$ lb loaf tin (pan) measuring 26 x 8 cm/10$^{1}/_{2}$ x 3 inches and 8 cm/3 inches deep with clingfilm (plastic wrap), pushing it right into the corners.

Ensure the gelato and sorbetto you are using have been churned or still frozen and then put in the freezer for the time stated in each recipe.

Line one-third of the tin with the *Gelato di Crema* and freeze the remainder for later. Fill a piping (pastry) bag fitted with a 1.5 cm/$^{5}/_{8}$ inch plain nozzle (tip) with the *Sorbetto di Mango* and, keeping your hands off the sides of the bag, pipe 2 lines along the layer of the custard gelato. Freeze for 30 minutes. Meanwhile, wash and dry the piping bag.

Spoon the remaining *Gelato di Crema* between the lines of mango sorbetto. Add about half of the remaining gelato to cover. Refreeze for 10 minutes. Fill the clean, dry piping bag fitted with the 1.5 cm/$^{5}/_{8}$ inch plain nozzle with the *Sorbetto di Lamponi* and repeat as for the mango. Freeze for 30 minutes.

Spoon some *Gelato di Crema* in between the lines of raspberry, then use the remainder to cover the top of the tin. Smooth over the top. Cover with clingfilm and freeze overnight.

To unmould, briefly dip the tin in hot water, wipe it and invert onto a tray. Give it a sharp shake and the block will flop out. Peel off the clingfilm, return to the freezer for 30 minutes, then cut into slices.

NEAPOLITAN

Many Italians were responsible for setting up gelaterias in Europe and the USA during the 19th century. These gelato makers came from Naples and the moulded ice cream blocks which became popular at the time were known as Neapolitan ice cream or mantanella *– layers of gelato frozen into a brick shape and sliced.*

The most common combination of flavours for these blocks was chocolate, vanilla and strawberry, but pistachio was also used. Here I've given my favourite combination, but you can try any concoction, including a mix of sorbetto and gelato. Traditionally, Neapolitan is made in layers, which are frozen in separate moulds then put together and refrozen, but this version is easier and gives the same effect.

Serves 6–8

$^1/_2$ quantity of *Gelato di Pistacchio* (p.103)

$^1/_4$ quantity of *Gelato di Crema* (p.78)

$^1/_2$ quantity of *Gelato di Fragole* (p.80)

Lightly oil and line a 1 kg/2$^1/_4$ lb loaf tin (pan) measuring 19 x 12 cm/ 7$^1/_2$ x 4$^1/_2$ inches and 8.5 cm/3$^1/_2$ inches deep with clingfilm (plastic wrap), pushing it right into the corners.

Ensure all the gelati you are using has been churned or still frozen and then put in the freezer for the time stated in each recipe. If any become too hard, then soften them in the fridge as recommended in the instructions.

Press thin scoops of the *Gelato di Pistacchio* into the prepared tin to form an even layer a little less than 3 cm/1$^1/_4$ inches deep and freeze for about 15 minutes. Add the *Gelato di Crema* in an even layer and freeze for 30 minutes. Finally, scoop the *Gelato di Fragole* onto the custard layer to a similar thickness and smooth the top. Cover with clingfilm and freeze overnight.

To unmould, briefly dip the tin in hot water, wipe it and invert onto a board. Give it a sharp shake and it will flop out, then remove the clingfilm. Put it back in the freezer for 30 minutes. Cut into slices and serve.

ZABAGLIONE PARFAIT GELATO

I serve this dessert in the summer months spooned into quenelles with perfectly ripe raspberries, and in autumn (fall) and winter I peel some little pears, leaving on their stalks and poach them in a Marsala-flavoured syrup. It is also used in the Tripolino below.

Serves 6–8

3 egg yolks

50 g/2 oz/¼ cup caster
  (superfine) sugar

50 ml/2 fl oz/¼ cup Marsala

250 ml/9 fl oz/generous 1 cup
  whipping cream

Whisk the egg yolks and sugar in a bowl until pale in colour then whisk in the Marsala. Sit the bowl over a saucepan of simmering water, making sure the bowl doesn't touch the water, and whisk until the mixture doubles in volume and becomes dense. Remove the bowl and put it in a larger shallow bowl of cold water, and continue to whisk until cool. Leave to chill for 10 minutes.

Whip the cream in a bowl until floppy and the same consistency as the egg mixture, then gently fold them together.

Transfer the mixture to the freezer for 4 hours. If it becomes too hard remove lid and transfer to the refrigerator 10 minutes before serving.

TRIPOLINO

I found the delightful Tripolino in Gelateria Petrini in Piazza dell'Alberone in Rome. Mauro Petrini, one of Italy's most skilled creators of gelato, told me his father named them so because they resembled the shape of the soldiers' hats in Tripoli. This is my version of his recipe, which is made with a zabaglione parfait, frozen in little moulds and dipped in luscious dark chocolate.

Makes 18

1 quantity of *Zabaglione
  Parfait* mixture (above)

300 g/10 oz plain dark
  (bittersweet) chocolate

Dariole moulds (see suppliers
  p.159)

Spoon the zabaione mixture into 50 ml/2 fl oz/¼ cup capacity dariole moulds. If using larger moulds just fill to a 50 ml/2 fl oz/ ¼ cup level and freeze overnight.

When the mixture has frozen firm, insert wooden lolly (popsicle) sticks or cocktail sticks (toothpicks), first dipped into hot water and dried, into the mixture. Re-freeze for a further 1 hour.

To unmould, dip the dariole moulds into hot water for 2 seconds, then dry them and ease out the ices using the stick. Arrange on a tray lined with greaseproof (waxed) paper and re-freeze.

Break the chocolate into a small heatproof bowl (so the chocolate when melted is deep enough to dip the Tripolino) and melt over a saucepan of hot water, making sure the base of the bowl is not touching the water. Remove the bowl and leave to cool slightly so the chocolate is still liquid.

Taking hold of the stick, dip the Tripolino, one at a time, into the cooled chocolate, coating the sides and top only, and letting the excess chocolate drip off. Put the stick between your fingers with the stick end of the Tripolino resting on the palm of your hand and pull out the stick. Put a palette knife under the Tripolino and transfer it to another greaseproof paper-lined tray. Re-freeze until ready to eat.

Orange Shell with Meringue

CONCHIGLIA D'ARANCIA CON MERINGA

This makes an extremely pretty dessert with very little effort and simple planning in advance makes it good for a dinner party. The orange shells freeze along with the sorbetto.

Serves 8

1 quantity of *Foglio di Meringa Italia* (p.153)

1 quantity of *Sorbetto di Flor di Arancia* (p.45)

8 orange shells, reserved from the making of the *Sorbetto di Flor di Arancia* (p.45), and frozen

Line a baking (cookie) tray with kitchen foil and fill a piping (pastry) bag fitted with a 1.5 cm/⁵/₈ inch star nozzle (tip) with half the meringue mixture. Pipe 8 turban shaped meringues onto the paper. These will keep in the refrigerator for about 6 hours (see Tip below for the remaining meringue mixture).

Fill the reserved, frozen orange shells with the sorbetto and freeze for 6 hours or overnight.

When ready to serve, place the tray of meringues under a hot grill (broiler) to brown them. Keep a close eye on them as the tops brown fast.

Take the sorbetto-filled orange shells from the freezer and, using a palette knife, lift one meringue at a time onto each shell. They will be a little soft on the base but it isn't difficult. Serve at once.

Tip: You can use up the remaining meringue mixture by piping small rounds onto a baking tray and baking them in a preheated oven 120°C/250°F/Gas Mark ¹/₂ for 1 hour. Allow them to cool completely and store in an airtight container.

ZUCCOTTO

Claudia Corsi of the Gelateria Combattenti in San Gimignano showed me how to make her version of this rich frozen trifle, a speciality of Florence, where the shape was inspired by the duomo *(cathedral dome) of the city. In the Tuscan dialect* zuccotto *means the cardinal's "skullcap".*

Serves 8

1 quantity of *Pan di Spagna* (p.154)

6 tbsp Strega

$\frac{1}{3}$ quantity of *Gelato di Cioccolato* (p.118), churned, frozen then softened slightly in the refrigerator, if necessary

$\frac{1}{2}$ quantity of *Gelato di Nocciola* (p.100), churned, frozen then softened slightly in the refrigerator, if necessary

10 Amarene cherries or any type of bottled cherries in syrup, drained and stoned (pitted)

$\frac{1}{2}$ quantity of *Semifreddo di Cassata* (p.124)

Line a 1.25 litre/2 pint/1 quart bowl with clingfilm (plastic wrap) leaving an overhang to turn over at the top. You will need to use almost all the *Pan di Spagna*. Cut it into triangles large enough to line the bowl (it doesn't need to fit perfectly) and using a pastry brush, brush both sides of each piece with the Strega. Press the soaked pieces into the sides of the bowl with the underside of the sponge facing outwards.

When the *Gelato di Cioccolato* is pliable, use it to cover the sponge in an even layer about 1.5 cm/$^5/_8$ inch thick, then freeze for 1 hour. Repeat with the *Gelato di Nocciola* and re-freeze for a further 45 minutes.

Fill the centre space with the cherries and spread the cassata on top. Cover by bringing the overhang of clingfilm up and over the top. Freeze overnight.

Unmould the *zuccotto* by dipping the bowl carefully into hot water to loosen the gelato a little. Wipe the bowl and loosen the clingfilm, then invert onto a small board or serving dish and ease the dessert out with the help of the clingfilm. Remove the clingfilm and wipe any melted gelato from around the base. Re-freeze for 10 minutes, then remove from the freezer and slice to serve.

FINAL TOUCHES

Gossips

CHIACCHERE

Known as frappe *in Rome, these little bits of frippery are just perfect for dipping into a bowl of soft gelato. They are really easy to make – bow shapes are often made in Italy.*

Makes about 28

Sunflower oil, for deep-frying

4 sheets of thin fresh lasagne,
    cut into shapes

Icing (confectioners') sugar, for
    dusting

Heat the oil in a deep-fat fryer to a temperature of 190–200°C/375–400°F, or use a deep sauté pan filled with 2–5 cm/1–2 inches of oil and keep adjusting the heat level to avoid the oil getting too hot. Deep-fry the lasagne shapes, about 5 pieces at a time, for about 1 minute until bubbly and crisp, but not brown.

Drain the pieces on kitchen paper (paper towels), and when cool dust with icing (confectioners') sugar. These can be made in advance and stored in an airtight container for up to 2 days. Dust with icing sugar just before serving.

Pear and Apple Crisps

RICCIOLI DI PERA E DI MELA

Makes about 24 crisps

3 ripe pears or
    6 red-skinned apples

125 g/4^{1}/$_{2}$ oz/^{5}/$_{8}$ cup caster
    (superfine) sugar

100 ml/3^{1}/$_{2}$ fl oz/generous
    ^{1}/$_{3}$ cup water

Preheat the oven to 120°C/250°F/Gas Mark ^{1}/$_{2}$. Line 2 baking (cookie) sheets with non-stick baking paper (baking parchment).

Finely slice the pears lengthways or the apples widthways using a mandolin. Put the sugar and the water in a frying pan (skillet) and heat gently to allow the sugar to dissolve. Increase the heat and boil for 3 minutes. Remove the pan from the heat and add the fruit slices. Leave them to soak for 2 minutes then take them out with a wide spatula letting the excess syrup drain off. Place the fruit slices on the prepared baking sheets and put in the oven to dry out – this will take about 2 hours. Turn them once halfway through the time, and don't let them brown. If they do start to brown turn the oven down.

When the fruit slices are dried out, remove from the oven and put on a wire rack to cool. They will crisp up as soon as they hit the air.

Little Meringues

BIANCHINI

Bianchini *means "little whites". Meringues are so useful for crushing into gelato or just eating with a sorbetto for a treat. Can be stored in an airtight container for up to 1 week.*

Makes about 30

3 large egg whites
Pinch of fine sea salt
200 g/7 oz/1 cup caster
 (superfine) sugar
50 g/2 oz/$^{1}/_{3}$ cup toasted
 hazelnuts, finely chopped

Preheat the oven to 140°C/275°F/Gas Mark 1.

Whisk the egg whites and salt together in a clean, grease-free bowl until just firm. Add the sugar, 2 tablespoons at a time, whisking well after each addition. Carefully fold in the hazelnuts so as not to lose the volume.

Fill a piping (pastry) bag fitted with a 2 cm/$^{3}/_{4}$ inch plain nozzle (tip) with the mixture, then pipe the mixture into mini paper cases. Bake in the oven for 30 minutes, then reduce the temperature to 130°C/250°F/Gas Mark $^{1}/_{2}$ and bake for a further 15 minutes. Leave to cool on a wire rack.

Caramelized Nuts

CROCCANTE

This is a useful little extra to sprinkle on top of gelato or crush down to a fine powder to add to a gelato mixture. If doing the latter simply deduct the amount of sugar used here from the recipe for the gelato.

Makes 1 x 20 cm/8 inch sheet

125 g/4$^{1}/_{2}$ oz/$^{5}/_{8}$ cup caster
 (superfine) sugar
3 tbsp water
125 g/4$^{1}/_{2}$ oz/$^{5}/_{8}$ cup toasted
 nuts, either pine kernels,
 almonds, hazelnuts or
 pistachio nuts

Line a baking (cookie) sheet with kitchen foil. Put the sugar and water in a small pan and gently heat to dissolve the sugar, about 4 minutes. Swirl the pan to dislodge any sugar crystals still on the bottom of the pan. Increase the heat to medium and let the syrup boil to a pale caramel colour. Add the nuts and stir to coat with syrup. Pour onto the prepared baking sheet and leave for 40 minutes until cool.

Break up into chards and store in an airtight container or a jar with a tight fitting lid for up to 1 month.

Iced Bowl

ZUPPIERA DI GHIACCIO

Vasi di Ghiaccio *or iced vessels, were fashionable at extravagant Medici banquets . These iced wonders were frozen solid in double moulds made from pewter. The inner mould was smaller than the outer one so the liquid to be frozen was poured into the gap between them, and clamped together to secure. The moulds were then put into tubs, filled with a mixture of icy snow and salt and more of this icy mixture was packed around them. The tubs were then placed in chilled cellars until the shapes were frozen into solid ice. Holes in the bottom of the tubs ensured that the snow would flow away as it melted and more fresh snow would be piled around the moulds. This was the art of the iced folly makers.*

To serve, either pile in scoops of sorbetto, or fill the bowl with finely crushed ice or snow and bury shot glasses, filled with pale sorbetto, in the ice. Use different flowers and leaves in whatever colours and shapes that are in the garden at the time. Bowls can be made months ahead and unmoulded for a special occasion.

2 freezerproof bowls (the inner bowl 2.5 cm/1 inch smaller all round than the outer. I used a bowl 1.5 litre/ 2¾ pints/4 cups for the outer and 700 ml/ 1¼ pints/3 cups for the inner)

Masking tape

Flowers, herbs and leaves of your choice

Wooden skewer

Clean cloth, for unmoulding

Fill the larger bowl with enough water so that the smaller bowl will float when immersed in the water. Secure the bowls together with an even amount of space all round with masking tape. Push the flowers, herbs and leaves into the water between the bowls with the help of a wooden skewer. Freeze for 1 hour to secure the flowers in place.

Top up with more water and flowers. Freeze overnight. If you want to speed up the process add ice cubes to the inner bowl.

To unmould, pour warm water into the small bowl and ease out using a clean cloth. To loosen the larger bowl, dip briefly into warm water and ease out the ice bowl. Return to the freezer until needed.

Tip: Use flowers that have not been sprayed with chemicals. Once out of the freezer, the ice bowl will last about 1 hour depending on the room temperature, but if the tray that it stands on is put in the freezer to get very cold beforehand, it will last even longer.

BISCOTTI

Use almonds or pine kernels instead of pistachio nuts, or a mixture of nuts. If you fancy chocolate biscotti add 25 g/1 oz sifted cocoa powder and use only 225 g/8 oz/1²/₃ cups flour.

Makes 40 thin biscotti or
   25–30 thick biscotti

250 g/9 oz/scant 1³/₄ cups
   plain (all-purpose) flour
175 g/6 oz/scant 1 cup caster
   (superfine) sugar
Pinch of salt
¹/₂ tsp baking powder
1 tsp aniseed (*arancini*) seeds
75 g/3 oz/scant 1 cup ground
   almonds
150 g/5 oz/1¹/₂ cups sliced
   pistachio nuts
2 eggs, roughly beaten
1 tsp vanilla extract

Preheat the oven to 200°C/400°F/Gas Mark 6. Lightly flour a baking (cookie) sheet. Put all the dry ingredients together in a large bowl and, using a wooden spoon, mix in the eggs and vanilla extract. Knead for a few minutes to make a paste. Cut into 2 portions and form each piece of dough into a 4 cm/1¹/₂ inch roll. Put the rolls on the prepared baking sheet and bake for 30 minutes. Lower the oven temperature if they overbrown. Transfer the rolls to a wire rack for about 25 minutes until cool enough to handle easily.

Slice the rolls thinly or thickly depending on what effect you prefer and put on 2 baking sheets. Bake for about 10 minutes until crisp but not golden. Lower the oven temperature if necessary to stop overbrowning. Leave to cool and store in an airtight container for up to 2 weeks.

Macerated Pomegranate Seeds

SETE AL LIQUORE

In Puglia pomegranates are known as sete, *meaning silk. Serve with the sorbetto on p.71.*

Serves 8

3 medium pomegranates
3 tbsp caster (superfine) sugar
3 tbsp Limoncello or an
   orange liqueur, such as
   Cointreau

Take the seeds from the pomegranates and put in a bowl. Mix the sugar into the liqueur and pour over the seeds. Leave to macerate for about 1 hour.

Italian Meringue Sheets

FOGLIO DI MERINGA ITALIANA

Meringa Italiana is produced by beating a hot sugar syrup into stiffly whisked egg whites, creating a very stable foam. These keep well, stored in an airtight container, for 1 month. If the air is damp they may go a little sticky when out of the container, so keep them covered until just ready to serve.

Makes 16

125 g/4^1/$_2$ oz/scant ^{2}/$_3$ cup
    caster (superfine) sugar
4 tbsp water
2 egg whites

Preheat the oven to 130°C/275°F/Gas Mark 1.

Put the sugar and water into a saucepan and gently heat until the sugar has dissolved, then increase the heat and boil to 121°C/250°F.

Meanwhile, whisk the egg whites in a clean bowl until they form soft peaks when the whisks are lifted out. Pour the hot syrup onto the whites in a steady stream, whisking all the time. Continue to whisk until the meringue has cooled and it is very stiff.

Line 3 baking (cookie) trays with baking paper (baking parchment) and using a palette knife smear the meringue mix into flat oblong shapes, about 15 x 7 cm/6 x 2^3/$_4$ inches. They do not have to be perfect or all the same – imperfections are good.

Bake for 40 minutes until a pale buff colour. If they seem to be still soft don't worry, as they will crisp as they cool. Taking one tray at a time, carefully peel and ease the sheets off the paper. If they stick just put them back in the oven for 5 minutes.

Store the meringues in an airtight container for up to a month.

Italian Sponge

PAN DI SPAGNA

This classic fatless sponge is used in many Italian desserts. It is used to form the shell of the moulded Zuccotto (p.145). Try making a tremezzini dolce *which is a lightly frozen sandwich made with layers of gelato and sponge, sliced and refrozen.*

Makes 1 sponge

3 eggs, separated
125 g/4^1/$_2$ oz/^{5}/$_8$ cup caster
    (superfine) sugar
^{1}/$_2$ tsp pure vanilla essence
75 g/3 oz/^{3}/$_4$ cup plain (all-
    purpose) flour
Pinch of salt

Preheat oven to 190°C/ 375°F/Gas Mark 5. Line a Swiss roll tin 26 x 38 cm/10 x 15 inches, 1.5 cm/^{3}/$_4$ inch deep with non-stick baking paper (parchment).

Put the egg yolks in a bowl with half the sugar and whisk until thickened. Add the vanilla essence and mix well. Sift the flour, 2 tbsp at a time, over the egg yolk and sugar mixture, gently folding through with a metal spoon.

In a clean bowl, whisk the egg whites with the salt until soft peaks form. Whisk in the remaining sugar, 1 tbsp at a time, until the mixture is stiff and glossy. Fold a little of the egg white mixture into the yolk and flour mixture to loosen it, then gently fold the remainder in. Spoon into the prepared tin, smooth the surface to make it even and bake in the oven for 15 minutes until firm and spongy to the touch.

Turn the sponge out onto a fresh piece of baking paper and transfer to a wire rack to cool (loosen it once to ensure it doesn't stick). If not using right away, wrap in more baking paper and then clingfilm (plastic wrap), and freeze. When ready to use, loosen the wrapping paper and defrost at room temperature for 30 minutes.

Ice Cubes

CUBETTI DI GHIACCHIO

Any flavour of gelato, sorbetto and juices, sweetened to your liking if you wish, can be frozen in any shape of ice cube tray (see right). Use the ice cubes whole, crushed in drinks or even blended into a smoothie.

INDEX

SUPPLIERS & EQUIPMENT

Gaggia Gelato maker
www.gaggia.co.uk

Magimix Ice Cream Machine
www.magimix.co.uk

**Chocolate truffle sticks and
chilli-flavoured chocolate**
www.theobroma-cacao.co.uk
020 8996 0431

**Vernaccia San Gimignano - Vin Santo and
Prosecco**
The Ultimate Wine Co. Ltd.
www.ultimatewines.co.uk
01628 472214

Orange and citrus peel
Sundora Foods
01759 302365
www.sundora.co.uk

Raspberry and strawberry liqueur
www.justminatures.co.uk
0870 7778017
www.bramleygage.com
01364 73722

Ice crusher and gelato containers
www.nisbets.com
0845 1405555

Gelato scoops
Continental Chef Supplies
www.chefs.net
0808 1001 777

Heat diffuser mat and simmer mat
Lakeland Limited
www.lakelandlimited.co.uk
015394 88100

Ice lolly maker
www.ukcookshop.co.uk
01273 832909

Ice lolly moulds
www.dexam.co.uk
01730 811811

Orange oil
Boyajian
www.boyajianinc.com

**Torrone di Mandorle (almond) and
Torrone di Pistacchi (pistachio)**
www.savori.co.uk
0870 2421823

Dextrose powder (glucose)
Nationwide at health shops and branches of
Boots or Waitrose

ACKNOWLEDGEMENTS

A huge thank you must go out to the many people who helped me so generously in the making of this book – without them it would not have been possible.

Firstly to Ruth Prentice, who inspired the writing of *Ices Italia* due to her lifelong love of gelato and for her support throughout.
To Jean Cazals for his beautiful photography and good company. He encouraged and instigated the project and never ceased to be enthusiastic and positive.
And to Kate Oldfield for taking it on.

Thanks also to all those who helped in the many exciting aspects of research and production:
Sue Rowlands for thoughtful styling and for giving 100%; Sergio Dondole, owner of Gelateria Di "Piazza", 4 Piazza della Cisterna, San Gimignano; Mauro Petrini, "gelatiere" and owner of Gelateria Petrini, Piazza dell'Alberoni, Rome; Giorgia Petrini for so kindly helping with translation; Nazzareno Giolitti of Giolitti, Via degli Uffici de Vicario, Rome; Claudia Corsi of Caffe Combattenti, Via San Giovanni, San Gimignano; Ben Hirst of Necci dal 1924 Pigneto, Rome, for much generosity; the team at Anova: Emily Preece-Morrison, Anna Cheifetz, Lotte Oldfield; Clare Barber for much useful help with research; Karen Beattie of the Ice Cream Alliance for kindly helping with a bombardment of questions. Paul Gayler, friend and supportive advisor on all things food; Philip Neal at Theobroma Cacao for chocolate advice; Georgina and Lucy Dawson for assisting and modelling; Robin Weir, co-author of the definitive book on Ices; Hamish Bain for encouragement and support; Craig Olsen for sensitive gelato testing skills, even though in New Zealand; Gabriella Le Grazie for so much help translating and getting me on the right track; Angela Boggiano; Mike Newton for knowledge of wines Italia; my sons Dan and Ben and Yumi for much diligent and enthusiastic tasting of "Ices Italia"; Roisin Neald for gelato feelings; Amanda Jensen Rolandini for help in all things; Massimo Pucci; Deborah Reeves.
Gelaterias: Doppia Coppia, Via Della Scala; Tre Scalini, Piazza Navona; Palazzo de Freddo di Giovanni Fassi, Via Principe Eugenio; Pallacchia 1900 Via Cola di Rienzo – all in Rome.
Luciano of Faubert's; Dan at Mortimer and Bennet; Andreas Georghiou & Co; Ugo Ginatta; Maria Bellachioma; Cecile Stern at Harrison Sadler; Amelia Ryde.

This edition first published in the United Kingdom in 2010 by
Pavilion Books
10 Southcombe Street
London, W14 0RA

An imprint of Anova Books Company Ltd

First published in hardback in 2007.

Design and layout © Pavilion, 2007
Text © Linda Tubby, 2007

Commissioning Editor: Kate Oldfield
Senior Editor: Emily Preece-Morrison
Home Economist: Linda Tubby
Photography: Jean Cazals
Stylist: Sue Rowlands
Copy Editor: Kathy Steer
Indexer: Patricia Hymans

ISBN 9781862059047

A CIP catalogue record for this book is available from the British Library.

10 9 8 7 6 5 4 3 2 1

Reproduction by Mission Productions Ltd, Hong Kong
Printed and bound by Toppan Leefung, China
www.anovabooks.com